Emory Richard Johnson

Inland Waterways, their Relation to Transportation

Emory Richard Johnson

Inland Waterways, their Relation to Transportation

ISBN/EAN: 9783742899231

Manufactured in Europe, USA, Canada, Australia, Japa

Cover: Foto ©ninafisch / pixelio.de

Manufactured and distributed by brebook publishing software (www.brebook.com)

Emory Richard Johnson

Inland Waterways, their Relation to Transportation

INLAND WATERWAYS,

Their Relation to Transportation.

BY

EMORY R. JOHNSON, PH. D.,

Instructor in Political and Social Science, at Haverford College.
Late Fellow of the Wharton School of Finance and Economy, University of Pennsylvania.

PHILADELPHIA:
AMERICAN ACADEMY OF POLITICAL AND SOCIAL SCIENCE.

CONTENTS.

CHAPTER.

I. Introduction. The Renaissance of Inland Navigation.

II. Classification of Inland Waterways. The Way They Should be Studied.

III. The Present Condition of England and American Inland Waterways.

IV. Waterways and Railroads as Carriers.

V. Influence of Inland Water Routes on Railroad Tariffs.

VI. Influence of Inland Waterways on Railroad Revenues.

VII. Under What Conditions and to What Extent Canals Can Compete With Railroads in the Future.

VIII. The Construction of Canals and the Improvement of National Inland Waterways by the State and by Corporations.

IX. Tolls on Waterways.

X. The Methods Employed by the United States in Improving and Extending Inland Waterways. The River and Harbor Bill.

XI. The Leading Works in the Process of Execution Within the United States. Proposed Works.

XII. The Nicaragua Canal.

XIII. The Economic Significance to the United States of the Extension of Inland Waterways.

CHAPTER I.

INTRODUCTION. THE RENAISSANCE OF INLAND NAVIGATION.

Transportation is a subject the importance of whose study needs little emphasis at the present hour. Such is the organization of industrial and social life that every person, be his activity great or small in the economic world, has a direct interest in the development and improvement of means of transportation. We no longer live the separated lives of former times, when each locality was sufficient unto itself. Society is becoming a unit and the industrial world a single complex body with manifold centres specialized for the performance of definite functions. When we speak of division of labor, of concentration and localization of industry, of clearing houses, of international exchange coinage and arbitration, we are simply giving names to certain phases of the movement toward social organization.

The thing most vitally essential to an organism consisting of many centres, or organs, having specialized functions upon the proper performance of which the welfare of the whole body depends, is the co-ordination of its various parts through their connection with each other by perfect means of communication. In this way only can each part receive from the others what is necessary to its fullest activity, and give in return those elements which make for the life of others. The higher and more perfect the organism the more complete must be the co-ordination of its parts. So with modern society. It requires the interchange of constantly increasing quantities of goods, and the connection of its many parts by efficient means of transportation and communication is a need that grows ever stronger. More than this, the expense of transporting these necessary goods becomes of greater moment to industry as processes of production are improved and costs are thereby reduced. For it will be readily seen that in one sense, at least, the analogy fails between an organism and the industrial society of the present time. In the case of the latter, most, though not all, special functions are given over, not to one, but to many industrial centres. Between these centres with like functions exists, in many cases, strong competition, each trying to take unto itself the greatest possible sum of advantages disregardful of the interests of others of its kind. In competitive industries, prices are forced down so low that but slight changes in the costs of transporting raw materials or finished products often mean life or death to business. Thus it is from the double source, from the growing need for the exchange of goods, and from the increasing significance of freight rates to the weal or woe of industry, that the importance of the transportation problem arises.

Turn where we will, we can but note the social and industrial effects of cheap rates of transportation. These results are in part beneficial, in part deleterious, always powerful. Cheap passenger rates have freed men from the chains that formerly bound them to the locality of birth, and have brought them into contact with the culture and science of our own and foreign lands. Cheap passenger and freight rates have effected great changes in population, have enabled people to increase rapidly in numbers, have opened up new lands to them, have gathered them into large centres of trade and industry. Cheap transportation in the United States has thrown open the West, and at the same time built up our great cities, and has, it is none the less true, made the crowded condition of life in them much worse by bringing to them the overflow of Europe and Asia to people the slums. The good we delight in has brought with it a train of evils whose extirpation social reformers are laboring to accomplish.

Paradoxical as it may seem, cheap and rapid transit is one of the strongest forces by which overcrowding and the other evils which together make up the low standard of life among the dependent classes are to be checked. The lower classes of society can be made independent only by raising their standard of life. This obviously requires two things, that the standard of life shall be made to include new articles of consumption, and that this enlarged standard shall become so firm that men will not lightly abandon it. The fulfillment of these requirements is made possible by cheap and rapid transportation, for it increases the number of articles that may compose the poor man's range of consumption, and in manifold ways directly and indirectly conduces to strengthen in him those intellectual and moral forces by which he will be impelled to introduce new articles of consumption into his standard of living.

It needs but a glance at the map for one to realize the significance of cheap rates to the industrial progress of the United States. Our wide boundaries include natural resources of great diversity. The raw materials of the farm and mine and forest must be carried to feed far-distant manufacturing industries, while the denser centres of population, still largely in the East, must obtain their food from the West. Considerations such as these alone enable us to comprehend the fact that the railroads of the United States annually transport nearly seven hundred million tons, and that the ton mileage of the traffic by rail is between eighty and ninety billion ton miles a year.

The carriers of freight hold the keys of trade. During the year 1890–91, over thirty iron smelting furnaces of eastern Ohio and western Pennsylvania were shut down several months, because the railroads could not give them a reduction of twenty-five cents a ton in the freight rates for coke fuel.* As slight a reduction as a mill a ton mile by the railroads in their charges would save to trade nearly a hundred million dollars a year.

The tonnage of inland waterways is not equal to the traffic by rail, but it is nevertheless enormous. Indeed, it

---

* *Cf.* Roberts, p. 10. Report on "The Respective Uses of Waterways and Railways in General Transportation in the United States," to the Fifth International Congress on Inland Navigation.

could hardly be otherwise with the presence within this country of such water-courses as the Hudson River, the Great Lakes, and the large rivers of the Mississippi Valley. On the Great Lakes there is a fleet of 3700 steam and sail vessels, with a net registered tonnage of 1,250,000 tons. In 1891, they carried 63,250,000 tons of freight, while in 1890, the ton mileage of the traffic carried by this fleet was 18,849,681,384 ton miles, or twenty-seven and a half per cent of the ton mileage of all the railroads of the United States. The commerce on the Great Lakes is advancing with rapid strides. The tonnage of the lake marine more than doubled during the five years from 1887 to 1892. In 1886, the net registered tonnage which passed through the St. Mary's Falls Canal was 4,250,000 tons. In 1890, it had risen to 8,250,000 tons; in 1892, to 10,000,000.

On the 16,000 miles of the navigable waters of the Mississippi River and its tributaries, there were afloat, in 1890, 7445 crafts of all kinds, with a registered tonnage of 3,400,000 tons. During the year, this fleet of boats carried 30,000,000 tons of freight and 11,000,000 passengers. The Hudson River had, in the same year, a traffic of 5,000,000 passengers and 15,000,000 tons of freight, exclusive of the 3,500,000 tons that passed from the State canals of New York, by way of the Hudson River to tide water. Adding these figures together, they give a total tonnage for these four waterways alone, of 112,916,223 tons. Such is the traffic on these waterways, while they are still practically separated from each other. A great increase would, of course, follow their connection by navigable ways of ample dimensions.

The Pennsylvania Railroad is the greatest freight carrier of any road in the world. During the year ending June 30, 1890, it carried on the 459 miles of its main line 69,036,245 tons; this same year the Reading's main line, 327 miles in length, had a traffic of 15,625,482 tons, and the New York Central and Hudson River Railroad had 29,473,879 tons of freight on its 849 miles. The total tonnage on these three great trunk lines, having a combined length of 1605 miles, was 114,135,558 tons, or an amount very nearly the same as that for the four waterways just named. If, however, the ton mileage statistics could be compared, the waterways would show a much larger ton mileage, because of the greater distance through which freight moves by water. The average distance which the freight was carried that passed the Sault in 1891, was 820.4 miles; the railroad freight of the United States moved on an average only 119.72 miles.

It is interesting to compare the inland navigation in the United States with the foreign trade. If 1889 be taken as the year for comparison, it will be seen that the total tonnage, entries and clearances, in the foreign trade at New York was 11,055,236 tons, and that the foreign trade for all the seaports of the United States taken together was 26,983,313 tons. The freight passing from Lake Huron to Lake Erie was estimated at about 20,000,000 tons; that is, the freight passing Detroit was twice the foreign trade of New York, and over two-thirds that for all our seaports together.

In considering these facts as to the inland navigation of the United States, it ought to be kept in mind that, with the exception of the lake marine, there have been, for several decades, but few improvements made in ways of navigating our inland waterways; whereas, the ocean steamship and the railroad have advanced rapidly in efficiency, one improvement following close on another. The extension of the inland waterways of the United States, during the last century, has kept pace neither with the development of maritime navigation, nor with the progress of the railroad. During the past fifteen years, we have been pursuing a liberal policy in the betterment of the natural water routes, but their extension and connection by means of canals have been neglected. Private interests have combined with public ignorance and apathy to prevent that development of the artificial waterways of the United States which is warranted by the magnitude of our inland commerce.

There has, indeed, been strenuous opposition to the policy which the United States has pursued in aiding inland navigation.* "Probably no class of general legislation," says Senator Frye, in the report of the Senate Committee on Commerce, "has been subjected to more severe and continued criticism than that enacted for the support and development of our internal and seaboard commerce by affording increased and safer means of communication." This opposition, of which Senator Frye speaks, has proceeded not only from railroads, but also from the demagogues of the press and stump, whose motives are seldom above reproach. There have been those, it is true, who in honesty of purpose and with words of wisdom, have raised a voice of warning against the methods which Congress has employed in its river and harbor legislation, and have urged Congress to pursue a policy not less liberal but more scientific. Such critics are deserving of gratitude rather than censure.

The expenditure of money for the construction of canals has been most strenuously opposed. The history and present condition of artificial waterways, and a misconception of their functions as agents of commerce, as it is carried on to-day, afford an explanation, though not a sufficient justification, for this feeling against the canal. In spite of this feeling, however, the magnitude and recent rapid increase in inland navigation, have not only strengthened the demand for the further improvement of natural waterways, but have also shown the necessity for supplementing these with canals. The large use that has been made of the ocean-ship canals, and of the purely inland waterways of France and Germany and New York, have increased this demand. The opposition to the liberal and scientific use of public money in the interest of inland routes of navigation will grow less; for, as Senator Frye says, "a more intelligent and clear perception of the results of such expenditure has been manifesting itself, and in all probability within the present century, as our inland and ocean traffic continues to

---

* For a fuller discussion of the opposition to appropriations for the aid of inland navigation than is here given, consult the author's paper on "River and Harbor Bills," ANNALS OF THE AMERICAN ACADEMY, Vol., II, p. 782. May, 1892.

develop and demonstrate each year more forcibly the wisdom and absolute necessity of our expenditures for rivers and harbors, the undeserved censure will have entirely ceased, and the only question to receive attention will be that of where the invariably adequate funds can be expended to the best advantage."

There is no doubt but that the growing favor in which the direct promotion by the State of inland navigation is regarded in the United States, France and Germany, is due in no small degree to the change which has taken place in men's conception of the functions of the State. The *laissez faire, laissez passer* theory is abandoned, and the direct intervention of the State in the affairs of trade and commerce for the purpose of adding to the wealth and welfare of society is to-day approved of under circumstances where it would have been condemned even a generation ago. Such being the attitude of men toward the State, attention is naturally turned to the inland waterways to see what is their commercial rôle, and to decide to what extent the State ought to participate in their improvement and extension.

The military significance of inland waterways has done not a little to turn attention to them and to enlist the State's interest in their construction. The growth of the feeling of nationalism that is so characteristic of the present, and of which the development of the military in every European country is but one manifestation, would and does do much to incite each nation to do all it can to improve the condition of its trade and industry, but the requirements of defence are an especially strong incentive to State aid to waterways. Prussia and the Empire are constructing the Nord-Ost-See Canal, very largely for the military purpose of securing a waterway from the Baltic to the North Sea through German territory. Our recent trouble with Chili did much to awaken the interest of the United States government in the Nicaragua Canal, and the feeling that the waterway ought to be controlled by the United States and by no other power is the reason that will ultimately induce the United

States government to aid or undertake the work. Those arguing for the construction by the United States of a lake ship canal from the Great Lakes to tide water never omit to score the telling point that such a waterway would be necessary to the defence of our frontier in case of a war with England.

Evidences of the renaissance of inland navigation are manifest in every country. In England, the Manchester ocean-ship canal is nearing completion, and other similar works of scarcely less importance are being discussed. France has been steadily enlarging and extending her inland waterways since 1879, and the much mooted project of making the Seine navigable for large ocean vessels as far as Paris seems reasonably sure of execution. Austria and Hungary are improving the Theiss and the Danube, and breaking down the "Iron Gates" that obstruct the commerce to and from the lower course of the Danube. Bavaria is considering the improvement of the Main and its connection with the Danube by a larger and more serviceable waterway than the existing canal. Besides aiding in the construction of the Nord-Ost-See Canal, Prussia is putting through a canal from the coal mines near the Rhine at Dortmund to the lower course of the Ems River, and has authorized the construction of other important canals. Rome and Brussels are especially interested in waterways, because of their desire to bring the ocean ships to their wharves.

The interest of the United States in the promotion of inland navigation is indicated by the numerous waterways conventions that have met during the last two years, and by the liberal appropriations which several successive Congresses have made. Private capital has begun the construction of the Nicaragua Canal, a work which the United States will doubtless aid if not entirely assume. A corporation is enlarging the Chesapeake and Delaware Canal into a waterway for ocean ships. Congress has appropriated large sums to continue the improvements of the Mississippi, Missouri, and Columbia rivers, and to deepen the channels of the

Great Lakes to twenty-one feet, and to begin the construction of an efficient waterway between the Great Lakes and the Mississippi River. Pittsburg is casting about to see whether she may not obtain connection with Lake Erie by means of a lake-ship canal; and the Minnesota Canal Company has recently been formed at St. Paul for the purpose of connecting St. Paul and Minneapolis by means of a similar waterway with Duluth and Lake Superior.

These and the many other works now being executed, or about to be begun, warrant the use of the expression—The renaissance of inland navigation. The works and projects referred to include not only the improvement of natural waterways, but also the construction of canals. The experience of the "Hepburn" investigating committee which the New York Legislature appointed in 1879, indicates the important place inland waterways, including the canal, have in transportation: "While the committee made no attempt to investigate the relations of the railroads to the canal, and sought to lessen their labors by avoiding this question, the canal, like Banquo's ghost, would not down; but we were compelled to meet it at every point and turn of the investigation."

CHAPTER II.

CLASSIFICATION OF INLAND WATERWAYS. THE WAY THEY SHOULD BE STUDIED.

Inland waterways may be divided according to the purposes they subserve, into three classes: First, natural waterways, of which there are two kinds: (1) Rivers and lakes whose commerce is distinct from that on the ocean in the sense that ocean vessels cannot navigate them, and (2) the lower courses of large rivers and the arms of the sea, whose waters float both ocean vessels and boats from the interior. Second, the inland canal, the purely artificial waterway whose purpose may be to lengthen a natural water-course, to connect separated rivers, lakes or arms of the sea, or to establish a waterway in a region where no water-course exists. Third, the ocean-ship canal, of which also there are two kinds: (1) Those such as the Suez Canal is, and as the Nicaragua Canal will be when completed, that shorten the routes of ocean travel and traffic. They are similar to the canal connecting two separated inland systems of navigation except that their purpose is rather to promote inland commerce indirectly, through facilitating carriage on the ocean, than directly by extending the routes of inland navigation. (2) The other class of ocean-ship canals are such as the Rotterdam, Amsterdam and Manchester canals, whose purpose it is to float ocean ships to the docks of cities that have previously been inland.

The maritime and lake-ship canal differ essentially from other artificial waterways. Their object is not only the transportation of goods a distance equal to their length, but also, in order that reloading may be avoided, to bear the ships containing the goods, either from one ocean, or large lake, to another or to some city that is a great manufacturing or distributing centre. The service they perform is a definite one; and one, too, that, as compared with the railroads, may be estimated in advance of construction with nearly as large a degree of accuracy, because of the fact that the railway can compete with such a canal in only a limited way and at a disadvantage. The probability that capital invested in such an enterprise will or will not yield a profit may be tolerably easily calculated. Maybe, the preliminary estimates of cost of the Manchester Canal fell far short of the actual expense of the work, while the experience of the Panama Company shows that over-credulous capitalists may be made the dupes of speculators and rogues in the case of waterway improvements, the same as in other enterprises. The failure of the Panama scheme was so obviously due to the fact that the undertaking became the gambling project of designing men that the future investment of capital in ocean-ship canals will not thereby be at all deterred. Economists and statesmen have united in advocating the construction of ocean-ship waterways since the Suez Canal gave such an impetus to commerce. The good returns yielded on capital invested have induced capitalists to undertake other similar works. The Manchester Canal is well on its way toward completion. The Nicaragua Canal has been begun and the success of the Suez Canal makes men well-nigh certain that these canals will be good investments of capital. The question, then, to be considered in connection with them is quite as much how and by whom they should be constructed as whether or not the works ought to be executed.

Of all countries in the world, the United States, because of its present and prospective commerce, has the most to hope for from maritime and lake-ship canals. We need in this country to study the actual commercial conditions, and in what way they can be bettered by these canals, and especially by the one at Nicaragua. The United States seems to stand before this project hesitating to enter upon it, much as the children of Israel stood at the entrance to the promised land and would not enter in. We, too, need some Joshua for a leader.

Many who concede the importance of maritime and lake-ship canals doubt whether the improvement of natural inland waterways and the construction of canals are works on which it is advisable, under present conditions, to expend capital. This phase of the question may, then, rightly be investigated at greater length. These two classes of undertakings, river improvements and canal construction, will not, nor should not as is done by some, be classified and discussed together. Because the improvement of important streams such as the Rhine and the Mississippi may, by reason of the commercial importance these rivers enjoy, be wise economy, it does not follow necessarily that canal building is worthy of promotion. Canals must be studied independently of rivers and be separately compared with railroads. That some one, the State or corporations, ought to improve the large lakes and more important rivers as commercial routes is granted by all. The relation that the government ought to bear to such works deserves further analysis than has yet been given the subject. The commercial importance of streams of secondary rank needs study in order to reveal what their real place is and ought to be in the transportation systems of the present time. As a result of the preliminary surveys of water-courses, which Congress in each river and harbor bill directs the United States Engineers to make, we have, in the "Annual Report of the Chief of Engineers," a large amount of material regarding the condition of the various water-courses of the United States and some information as to their commerce.* The statistics of the inland navigation of the United States are, however, still very incomplete. The eleventh census is the first one that has undertaken to gather, compile and publish full statistics concerning all classes of transportation by water, and, with the exception of the Great Lakes, Lake Champlain and the rivers of the Mississippi Valley, this has given us no

---

* In 1890, Major H. M. Adams, of the United States Engineer Corps, prepared, in the office of the Chief of Engineers, an outline map of the United States, showing the tonnage of the rivers and harbors of the United States. This work has not been repeated since.

statistics of inland navigation as distinct from the coast-wise traffic. There ought to be legislation enacted by Congress providing for the collection, classification, and compilation of full and reliable statistics of the inland commerce of the United States. Perhaps we shall secure this when Congress establishes a permanent bureau of statistics. The United States Engineers have given us data enough to show that streams of secondary importance have a place in our transportation system; we need, however, to classify these statistics and to investigate in a broader and more comparative manner the commercial industrial and economic effects of these streams and to inquire how and by whom the expenses of carrying this on are to be met.

To ascertain the position the canal occupies in the commercial and industrial world is not easy. If "specialists, even, have the greatest difficulty in holding that tight rein on their thought without which it is impossible to arrive at an independent judgment," we can hope to get at a true solution of the problem before us only by a careful historical and statistical study. The present condition of the canal, and the progress which engineering science is now making in rendering the canal a more efficient agent, need to be given a careful consideration in the investigation which this monograph proposes to make.

To state the problem broadly, it is necessary, in order to answer the question—What is the present and what may be the future importance of inland waterways?—to find out their present condition, and how much freight is carried on them and on the railroads, to ask what influence inland waterways exert on railroad tariffs and revenues, to inquire especially under what condition and to what extent canals can compete with railroads in the future. To make this discussion complete it is necessary to decide to what extent the State should construct canals and improve inland waterways, and how far the State ought to leave this work to corporations, and to treat the question of tolls on State waterways. Having done this, the peculiar needs of the United States and what is being done to meet them may be profitably studied. To accomplish all this is admittedly a task at once difficult and important.

The question whether inland waterways shall be improved cannot be answered alike for all countries. In these States where both railroads and waterways are owned and controlled by the government, the problem is simpler. Waterways will be found to have an important influence on railroad charges even under these circumstances; but the waterways are to be regarded less as competitors and more as complements of the railroads. The problem in such countries is to discover how the two carriers may best be made to co-operate as parts of a single unified system of transportation. In countries such as the United States, France and England, where the railroads are private property under private control, the influence of navigation on railroad tariffs calls for more detailed study. In this case waterways must regulate railroad rates chiefly by competition, and how to maintain the navigable ways as independent competing routes becomes a vital question. It should still be the purpose of the State to form of the two carriers a single system of transportation, the difference between the relation of waterways—private or State—to State railways and to private railways being that in the latter case the two parts of the system should compete with each other, while in the former instance this is not necessary.

Most of all it is essential in considering the relative merits of railroads and improved waterways that one's mind be kept free from prejudices. The question of improving waterways and constructing canals affects favorably and unfavorably large money interests. Business men often argue on the basis of their own individual advantage. Engineers sometimes approach the question more regardful of their present and future reputation than of the real merits of the discussion. Legislators, especially under our system of making improvements, are frequently too strongly influenced by personal and local interests, and do not give due weight to national considerations. The investigator of an economic problem such as this should not approach the question as an advocate of the waterway, nor as a friend of the railway, but as a seeker after truth. His attitude should be one of unbiased inquiry.

CHAPTER III.

THE PRESENT CONDITION OF ENGLISH AND AMERICAN INLAND WATERWAYS.

The policy of the federal government toward the improvement of rivers and harbors during the past fifteen years has been liberal. The deepening of harbors has been generously cared for, and the Great Lakes and the Mississippi River have been treated in a like manner; but the construction of canals to connect the more important systems of waterways with each other and to the ocean has not been so vigorously pushed. Indeed, the construction of canals in the United States, either by the States or by the Federal Government has stood practically at a standstill for a generation. Those waterways that were once the pride of the States, have either been abandoned by their owners, or allowed to fall into a condition of little usefulness.

The present condition of inland waterways is easily accounted for. The rôle that the canal is to-day called on to play in commerce, differs from its rôle of sixty years ago. Most canals existing at present were constructed at a time when industrial needs existed that have since greatly changed or passed away. They were constructed when the volume of freight seeking movement was comparatively small, and when through, as contrasted with local, freights was relatively unimportant. The localization and centralization of industries, and the concentration of population into great manufacturing centres had but begun. Industry did not then as now call for the movement of great quantities of bulky raw materials long distances, but rather for the carriage of small quantities to less remote points. The canals of England and the continent generally were built accordingly. Numerous corporations constructed small waterways with dimensions sufficient only to meet the needs of the time. Very little regard was paid by one canal company to the dimensions of waterways other than their own. In the United States, most canals were longer and looked to the movement of traffic greater distances, but they were small and calculated only for the movement of small volumes of freight.

The railroad also entered the transportation field when traffic was largely local in character and still small in amount. The first railroads were short local lines. They began competing with the waterway for a traffic which they soon showed themselves better able to handle; for the railroad is an agent better adapted than the waterway to the transportation of small quantities of goods a short distance. The railroad conquered in the early contest with the canal and the improved river, and what is more, during this contest an important industrial change was going on in society. This alteration in industrial conditions was partly due to the influence of the railroad, partly caused by other inventions, and not a little accelerated by the awakened intellectual activity, and the increase in the scale of human wants that have accompanied the change. This transformation has put quite a new phase on the commercial needs of society. There has been a great revolution in transportation. Passenger traffic has reached such immense proportions that those of fifty years ago seem insignificant. Freight has not only enormously increased, but has radically changed in character, a fact of which the great trunk lines of the United States are a striking example. The railroad has made possible the rapid growth of large cities, and the concentration of manufacturing into great centres. The food supply of the cities of the eastern part of the United States and of those of England even is drawn from the grain fields of the Mississippi Valley. In determining what is the function of inland waterways in commerce, these facts must be kept in mind.

To enter at length into the history of the struggle of the railway and waterway that brought about the present condition of the canal would take this discussion too far afield.* But while we are especially concerned with present conditions we may with profit refer to the past when such references help explain present conditions and aid us in deciding what policy ought to be adopted in the future. The purpose being rather to accomplish this than to cover the history of the relation of the railway and waterway in a complete manner, it will be sufficient to bring out the salient facts of the struggle in England and in America. England being the only country where the waterways and railroads were and are both private property, her experience is especially instructive.

The contest between the waterways and railroads of England was very bitter. When the railroad strove to enter the field there was great opposition on the part of the canal companies. They were sole possessors of commerce. There was very little competition among canal companies, they held monopolies and charged excessively high tariffs.† The first railroad charter of importance was granted in 1826 for a line between Manchester and Liverpool. The two canals connecting these places had pooled and raised their charges exorbitantly high. They opposed the request of the railroad company for a charter so strongly that it cost Huskisson $350,000 to get the act through Parliament. The Manchester and Liverpool railroad was a great success and railroad building progressed rapidly. The contest with the waterways raged inside and outside of Parliament, and the canals were not long in losing their overpowering strength. As pointed out above, the railroads were a better commercial

* For a full account of the struggle in England, see Cohn's "*Englische Eisenbahnpolitik.*" An account for France and England is briefly given in Hadley's '*Railway Transportation.*" The text of all the important English laws for the regulation of railways is given in the "Second Annual Report of the Interstate Commerce Commission."

† *Cf* a speech by Morrison in the House of Commons, May 17, 1836: "The history of existing canals, waterways, etc., affords abundant evidence of the evils to which I have been adverting. An original share in the Loughborough Canal, for example, which cost 142£ 17s. is now selling at about 1250£ and yields a dividend of 90£ or 100£ a year! The fourth part of a Trent and Mersey Canal share or 50£ of the company's stock, is now fetching 600£, and yields a dividend of about 30£ a year. And there are various other canals in nearly the same situation." Hansard's Debates, 3d. Series, Vol. xxxiii., p. 981.

agent for the carriage of most kinds of freight then seeking transportation, and though built chiefly like canals to carry on a local traffic, they quickly and easily adapted themselves to the transportation of through freight. They kept pace with the revolution in industry and commerce, because they readily admitted of extension, unification, and consolidation. Not so the canals of England, whose dissimilarity of dimensions made combination difficult, and prevented competition to any great extent with the railroads for long-distance traffic. They did not keep abreast of the progress of events. The owners of the canals were, of course, largely to blame; for they did not understand that with the advent of the railroad the function of the canal changed, nor did they push forward the improvements in waterways that were necessary to adapt them to the altered industrial and commercial interests. Vested interests are by nature always conservative.

The railroads were alert and several circumstances were favorable to them. Most of the industrial cities had grown up along the lines of the canals, and thus it was that many railroads paralleled the canals and came into competition with them. No attempt was made by either party, as has since been done, to share freights in order that each might take the part it was by nature best fitted to transport, but various methods were adopted by the railroads to injure the efficiency of their rivals. The canal lines, as has been said, were composed of several parts, each section being in the ownership of an independent company. The railroad company had only to buy a short section, if it were an important one, to get possession of a whole line. This it did, and the canals or sections so purchased were frequently repaired in the busy season, and were often closed for traffic during the night. When the waterway was parallel to the railroad, rates on the latter were made lower. Furthermore, it was of advantage to the railways that canal companies were not allowed, till 1845, to be shippers, and that canal freight rates were fixed by the government. The railroads had neither of these governmental restrictions. Some canals and railroads ended competition by uniting in trusts. Other owners of waterways strove, but unsuccessfully, to form independent trusts; thus canal property declined rapidly and its absorption by the railroads continued.

By these means the railroads were able the more quickly and more fully to cripple the waterways. These circumstances, however, only hastened a result that must surely have ultimately followed. The canals of England were doomed to defeat from the moment of their entry into competition with the railroads in the general field of transportation; and for several reasons: The railway lines, at least after the first few years, were much longer than the competing waterways; thus the canal companies with small quantities of capital had to compete with the larger amounts of capital owned or controlled by the railroad corporations. Again, the canals could carry only freight, while the railroads conveyed passengers as well. The policy of the railroads, very naturally, was to keep passenger rates high and to cut on freight charges till competition on the part of the canals became impossible. Of course the railroads were not obliged to cut on all freight. All fast freight came to them in any case, and it was only on slow, bulky goods that they needed to lower rates to embarrass the canals. The last two of these reasons are as valid to-day as they were then and are quite sufficient to demonstrate the fact that the field of the waterway in transportation is a narrower one than that of the railway. What that field is and what its importance is will be the subjects of later inquiry.

The legislation of Parliament has done but little in aiding the development of canals and their maintenance as competing waterways. The numerous petitions from railway companies for charters kept the relation of the State to railroads and canals, and the relation of the two means of transportation to each other constantly before Parliament during the early decades of railroad building. The necessity for governmental control of railroad charges was not at first realized. It was thought that canals and railroads would compete and keep down charges, and it was also generally supposed that on railroads the same as on turnpikes shippers would compete with each other. The Select Committee of the House of Commons that reported in 1839 was the first to recognize the fact that the owners or operators of a railroad must necessarily control the shipment of goods, and that it was impracticable for individual shippers to own and run cars and engines in the way they had used their own boats and wagons on canals and turnpikes. The following year the Select Committee of the House of Commons declared itself to be "aware that instances are not wanting where companies and large capitalists, instead of competing, have combined and entered into agreements whereby the public have suffered," but still it did not consider it had material enough to judge itself able to establish a schedule of maximum rates. It thought the canals might be looked to to control rates on heavy articles, but could not deny that the tendency of canals also would be to combine with the railroads rather than to compete against them.

The power of the railroads rapidly grew strong in Parliament. A resolution introduced into the House of Commons, by Mr. Morrison, 1836, for the governmental revision of rates each twenty years, met at first with approval in Parliament, but soon encountered such an opposition from railroad interests as to defeat it. In 1844, Mr. Gladstone, at that time president of the Board of Trade, said, "The railway interest is, perhaps, the strongest in regard to direct influence on votes of members."* The bill which passed in 1844, stipulating that railroads constructed in the future might be purchased by Parliament after they had been operated twenty-one years without interference, and had yielded a profit annually of ten per cent for three years previous to purchase, had, of course, placed no real control over

* Speech in Parliament, July 8, 1844. Hansard's Parliamentary Debates, third series, Vol. lxxvi., p. 493.

the actions of railroad companies. In 1845, the canal companies petitioned Parliament for protection against the competition of the railroads, and secured, for the first time, the right of becoming shippers over their own canals, and obtained the power to raise and lower their tariffs. The canal companies were now, for the first time, on equal legal footing with the railroads.*

Reasons have been given that explain why simple legal equality of the canal and railway companies was insufficient guarantee that canals would or could maintain themselves as independent agents of commerce. Railways continued to combine with each other and to get the canals, either by purchase or consolidation, more and more under control. Parliament investigated the matter, and in 1847 established a well-nigh powerless Railway Commission, which existed till 1851, without accomplishing anything. In 1852, the House appointed a select committee " to consider the principle of amalgamation as applied to railway, or railway and canal bills, and to consider the principles which ought to guide the House in railway legislation." The committee found that in several important districts the canals and railroads had united; that the absorption of canal property by the railroads had not been checked, and that the parliamentary regulation to secure freedom of traffic on the canals had been ineffectual.† The result of the investigation was the "Act for the Better Regulation of the Traffic on Railways and Canals," 1854; Section 2 of which enunciated several provisions that have appeared in most subsequent English and American laws for the control of railroads. It may, indeed, be said that it has been the ideal of railroad legislation since 1854 to give validity to the provisions of this section. It provides: " Every railway company, canal

---

* "Only ten of the sixty or seventy canal navigation proprietors (1892) in the United Kingdom act as carriers." Edwin Clements, in article on " Taxes and Tolls of the United Kingdom." Report to Fourth International Congress on Inland Navigation.

† Reference is here made to only such part of the committee's report as concerns the discussion in hand.

company, and railway and canal company shall, according to their respective powers, afford all reasonable facilities for the receiving and forwarding and delivering of traffic upon and from the several railways and canals belonging to or worked by such companies respectively, and for the return of carriages, trucks, boats and other vehicles, and no such company shall make or give any undue or unreasonable preference or advantage to, or in favor of, any particular person or company, or any particular description of traffic, in any respect whatsoever; nor shall any such company subject any particular person or company, or any particular description of traffic, to any undue or unreasonable prejudice or disadvantage in any respect whatsoever; and every railway company, and canal company, and railway and canal company having or working railways or canals, which form a continuous line of railway or canal or railway and canal communication, or which have the terminus, station, or wharf of the one near the terminus, station or wharf of the other, shall afford all due or reasonable facilities for receiving and forwarding all the traffic arriving by one of such railways or canals by the other, without any unreasonable delay, and without any such preference or advantage, or prejudice or disadvantage as aforesaid, and so that no obstruction may be offered to the public desirous of using railways or canals, or railways and canals as a continuous line of communication, and so that all reasonable accommodation may, by means of the railways and canals of the several companies, be at all times afforded to the public in that behalf." The law also provided that complaints of aggrieved parties were to be brought in the Court of Common Pleas, and this was quite sufficient to make the law without effect. In twenty years only two suits were brought to enforce the stipulation in regard to the shipment of goods, and both cases were lost. The rulings of the courts as to the meaning of undue preference and unreasonable rates were so liberal as to deprive the law of nearly all force.

The relation of the waterways and canals of England has not materially changed since 1854. In 1872 the means of communication were again investigated at length by another Select Committee of the House of Commons. The report made was only negative in character as regards the policy to be pursued in legislating on inland waterways. The committee reported that when Parliament had permitted canals to unite with railroads the conditions which she had imposed to secure the maintenance of the canals in a navigable condition had been easily avoided. If Parliament were to prohibit the canal companies from selling out to, or uniting with, the railroads, the competition of the railroads would bankrupt the canal companies. Again, if a canal company came to Parliament asking permission to sell out in order to avoid bankruptcy what was to be done except to grant the request? The committee thought nothing short of State purchase of canals would be able to preserve them as competitors of the railroads, and such a policy the committee did not feel warranted in recommending.

The bill of 1873, "An Act to Make Better Provision for Carrying into Effect The Railway and Canal Traffic Act, 1854, and for other purposes connected therewith," resulted from this investigation. It established a Railway Commission consisting of three members and two assistants, in whose hands was placed the enforcement of the law of 1854. The law stipulated (Section 14) that "Every railway company and canal company shall keep at each of their stations and wharves a book or books showing every rate for the time being charged for the carriage of traffic other than passengers and their luggage from that station or wharf to any place to which they book, including any rate charged under any special contract, and stating the distance from that station or wharf of every station, wharf, siding, or place to which any such rate is charged." The commissioners were empowered to decide whether terminal charges were reasonable. No railroad company was permitted except by statutory permission from Parliament to purchase or to obtain control of a canal without consent of the commissioners.* Thus the law

* The law was to be in effect only five years, but in 1878 it was continued till the end of 1879, then till December 31, 1882, then for three years longer, when the commissioners were made a permanent body.

strengthened the degree of the State's supervision and was a step in the right direction. The commissioners did not secure low rates for shippers, the law did not by any means cure the evils of unequal and excessive charges by the railroads; but the commissioners did constitute a court before which many railroads guilty of unjust and unequal charges were brought and made to change their tariffs. The law did not bring about a revival of inland commerce, and the foregoing discussion has given reasons amply sufficient to show the impossibility of that taking place on the canals as constructed seventy and a hundred years ago. Though from 1873 to 1882 the commissioners' power of compelling a railroad owning canals to maintain its waterway in a navigable condition was exercised only once, still the position of the canals as compared with the railroad was a more favorable one. They did not prosper very much, but they held their own.

The revival of interest in inland navigation has been especially marked since 1880, and this was very largely the cause of an attempt by Parliament in 1888, to pass such a law as would surely enable the waterways of England to develop and enter more fully into competition with the railroads. The condition of inland navigation in England is at present not entirely discouraging. The canals have not been entirely driven to the wall. The map of England shows a complicated network of canals and canalized rivers whose length is 3813 miles. Of canal companies proper, there are in England thirty-nine, in Scotland none, and in Ireland five. Of public trusts which control canals or canalized rivers as municipal or county conservancy boards, commissions, or trusts there are thirteen in England, two in Scotland, and five in Ireland. Three city corporations of England are proprietors of navigations, and five canals of England are owned by private individuals. The number of railway companies owning canals in England are fifteen, in Scotland two, and in Ireland one, and they own or control no less than 1375 of the total 3813 miles of the waterways of the United Kingdom.* This last fact presents the most important and most difficult phase of the problem. In spite of the past legislation, the railways control a large share of the English canals; indirectly, they dominate many more. This indirect control comes about in two ways. On the one hand from the fact that the railway-owned canals often constitute parts of longer lines, and on the other hand, because the railroad, on coming into competition with the canals, has influenced them to confer in fixing rates.

The more important provisions of the railway and canal traffic act of 1888, by which it is hoped to free the canals further from the domination of the railroad and maintain them as competitors, are as follows : The Railway Commission was superseded by a Railway and Canal Commission, consisting of two commissioners appointed by Her Majesty, and three ex-officio commissioners. The three ex-officio members are judges of a superior court, England, Ireland and Scotland each having one of the three. In England, by the Lord Chancellor; in Scotland, by the Lord President of the Court of Sessions, and in Ireland, by the Lord Chancellor of Ireland, the judge is designated who shall serve for a period of at least five years as ex-officio railway and canal commissioner. The commissioners are given a greater control over rates. They can (Section 31,) on the application of any one interested in through traffic, order through rates, and decide whether any proposed rate is just and reasonable. Formerly they could act only on the application of a canal or railway company. The navigation owners must make yearly reports to the Board of Trade and the Registrar of Joint Stock Companies regarding the capital, revenue, traffic and capacity of their navigations. No canal can be closed for more than two days without previously notifying the Board of Trade. By Section 42, no railway company is allowed to acquire any interest in canals without previously securing statutory authority therefor. Every

* *Cf.* "Taxes and Tolls on Inland Navigation in the United Kingdom," pp. 5-6. Edwin Clements' Report to the Fifth International Congress on Inland Navigation.

canal company is required (Section 39) to submit revised classifications and schedules of rates and tolls to the Board of Trade, and these schedules are to be submitted to Parliament for revision.

Parliament has revised the schedule of maximum rates which the railroads may charge for the conveyance of merchandise traffic. In May, 1892, the Board of Trade began the investigation of the powers of navigation companies and their rate charges; the schedules have been revised by the Board of Trade, but have not yet been acted on and put in force by Parliament. As the first step in this investigation the board, in pursuance of Section 39 of the law, required statistical information from each canal and navigation company, and it was found that the paid up capital invested in canals and navigations, not owned by the railroad companies is about $100,000,000. The railway companies owning canals do not separate the capital invested in waterways from their other capital. The total traffic on all the inland waterways of the United Kingdom reaches the considerable sum of 36,301,120 tons. The waterways of Scotland are the only ones showing actual loss on investment; those of England and Wales not owned by railway companies netted the low profit of 2.76 per cent; if Scotland and Ireland be included, the average falls to two and a-half per cent.

Concerning the operation of the law of 1888 it is still rather early to judge. One thing, however, may be asserted; should the law result in making competition possible between rail and water traffic it will only prepare the way for the revival of inland navigation. The inland navigation routes of England must most of them be reconstructed before they become effective agents of modern commerce. This will mean in many cases the enlargement and improvement of existing routes, in some cases the location of new ones, and doubtless the abandonment of many old ones. The causes that have brought about the present condition of English waterways have been cited here because they seem especially instructive. From England's experience with waterways under private ownership we may learn much by which to guide our action in the future. The conclusion that we may rightly draw is not necessarily that the State ought to own the waterways. That the State must, however, closely supervise the location, construction, and operation of both waterways and railroads when both are owned by corporations, if it wishes to maintain the waterways as competitors of the other routes, seems to be a fact strongly emphasized by the experience of England.

The present condition of the inland waterways in the United States is partly explained by the history of their construction and partly by the industrial changes that have taken place since the introduction of the railroad. These changes have made the competition of railroads more ruinous to the waterways. The larger natural waterways of the United States are playing an increasingly important rôle in our commerce, while most of the old canals have lost their former commercial significance. The mania for canal building seized the States after the successful completion of the Erie canal, in 1825. New York, Pennsylvania, Ohio, Indiana, entered upon the construction of extensive works of internal improvement, and other States aided private enterprise with large contributions of money. In most States private companies, usually with State aid, constructed canals of more or less importance.*

The total length in 1880, of the canals in the United States was 4468 miles. They had cost $214,041,802. Of these canals, 1953 miles had been abandoned, leaving the length of those in operation 2513 miles.† The only States owning or aiding canals at present are New York, Ohio and Illinois. The other States have quite ceased to aid internal improvements. Most of the canal property they once owned

---

*I have purposely avoided going at length into the early history of water communication in the United States, but have inserted in the bibliography at the end of the monograph those books that I have found useful in studying the subject.

† *Cf.* Report on Canals of the United States. Tenth Census, Vol. iv.

has been abandoned or sold to private corporations, while a few important ones have been turned over to the Federal Government. Such was the case with the St. Mary's Canal, constructed by the State of Michigan, and later, in 1880, handed over to the United States. The reason why the Federal Government has taken such canals from the States, and the same is true of the many river improvements that have passed from the States to the United States, is not because the unprofitable character of such works made the States desirous of being rid of them, but primarily because the national importance of the waterways made it preferable that their improvement, and the control of them should be the charge of the Federal Government rather than of the States.

One of the causes why the States ceased making internal improvements and sold or abandoned their canals was the financial panic of 1837. Many States had gone heavily into debt in constructing canals and improving waterways, and the financial storm left them stranded. They were bankrupt and had to cease their works of internal improvement. More than this, they found the works that had been executed to be in many cases a burden to their treasury, and not a source of income. This was partly due to the fact that the canals had not always been well located, and that too many had been built; but more because of the war of the railroads against the waterways. The canals were mostly located while the industries of the States were yet young. When the States developed, the movement of freight was often not in the direction of the canals, and this left to the waterways only the comparatively unimportant local traffic. The canals, poorly located and ill-adapted to perform large commercial services, were unable, in most cases, to hold their own against the railroads. The war of the railroads on the waterways was, very naturally, no less incessant here than in England.

The length of the abandoned canals, both private and State, is large. The canals in the New England States were private property, and they have all been abandoned for commercial purposes.* New York has abandoned 356 miles of lateral canals, in Pennsylvania 477 miles have ceased to be used, Ohio has abandoned 205 miles, and Indiana 379 miles. †

The competition of the railroads of Pennsylvania resulted in the sale of the canals to the Pennsylvania Railroad and the Sunbury Railroad in 1857 and 1858. Ohio leased her canals in 1861 to a corporation for a period of ten years at an annual rental of $20,775. They were again leased in 1871 for another period of ten years; but in 1877 the lease was given up because the State had allowed the destruction of a reservoir at Hamilton, Ohio. From December, 1877, to May, 1878, the canals were in the hands of a receiver, and then they were again placed under the management of the State Board of Public Works. The State now operates them and charges tolls for their use.

In general it may be said that New York, and, to a less degree, Illinois, are the only States that stood by their water-ways at the critical period of their history. That critical time came when the old waterways, adapted to the needs of the commerce of the third and fourth decades of this century, ceased to be fit routes for the traffic of the succeeding years when reconstruction and development were absolutely essential to their future usefulness. New York did this in a measure at least, and her waterways are of comparative importance. Other States pursued a different policy. Pennsylvania, as was seen, sold out her plant; Ohio leased hers for a song; Illinois was apathetic; the other States that had been aiding private enterprise ceased to make further contributions.

The abandonment of many lines of State and private canals was wise. The canal mania had led to many injudicious constructions, and changes in commercial conditions incident to our rapid industrial development deprived others of their

---
* They were about two hundred miles long, and, with the exception of the Middlesex Canal, of only minor importance.

† *Cf.* Tenth Census, Vol. IV.

usefulness. The choice that confronted the States lay between selecting and improving the more important routes, and abandoning all of them either to disuse or the ownership of corporations whose interests were not those of the general public. With the exception of New York and Illinois, the latter course was followed, and with results such as were anticipated.

The present condition of the canals in the United States need not be dwelt on at length. The principal canals of Pennsylvania are owned by the Pennsylvania Railroad and the Reading Railroad, and these companies have thus far found it to their own interest to add to the large railroad plant which they owned at the time of the acquisition of the canals and to make the greatest possible use of that, rather than to undertake such a reconstruction of the waterways as will make them really efficient agents of transportation. They have had "no spur to prick the side" of their intent. The chief freight that the canals of Pennsylvania transport is coal. As the Reading Combine practically controls the coal output, it fixes the price for transportation far above the costs of moving by rail.* The principal canal of Ohio is the Miami and Erie, connecting Cincinnati and Toledo. Its dimensions are not only small, but dissimilar in different parts of the waterway. From Cincinnati to Dayton, a distance of sixty-five miles, it is forty feet wide and four feet deep; for the next 114 miles, that is, from Dayton to Junction, it is fifty feet wide and five feet deep; from Junction to Toledo, sixty-four miles, the width is sixty feet and depth six feet. Between Toledo and New Bremen, in the middle of the State, there are forty-nine locks to effect a rise of only 118 feet. The locks, furthermore, are only eighteen feet wide and sixty feet long, the construction, including the gates, being of wood.

Even New York has not of late sustained her former liberal policy, and the condition of her canals is justly the subject of

* There is some indication that the Schuylkill Canal is to be improved, because the Reading is unable to handle the coal demanded for the Philadelphia market

complaint. In his report for 1891 the Superintendent of Public Works, of New York, calls the attention of the Legislature to the fact that there are many improvements needed, and then adds: "It should be remembered that, with the single exception of lock-lengthening, and the ordinary repairs, no improvements nor extensions have been made to the canals since 1856. The improvements are entirely inadequate for the purposes for which they were intended, and additional improvements must be made without delay if the canal system of the State is to be preserved in all its usefulness."

This somewhat lengthy discussion of the canals of England and the United States prepares the way for considerations that are to follow. The waterways of France and Germany, which are in a much better condition will be referred to in the next chapter. The present backward condition of English and American inland waterways, especially canals, will not be remedied until the people of the two countries arrive at a truer conception of the real commercial functions of the waterways, and what is necessary for the exercises of those functions. The present and future differ from the past. "Canals as they were a century ago have no longer any function to fulfill that is worthy of serious consideration. Their mission is ended, their use is an anachronism. The canals of the future must be adapted to the new conditions of commerce." *

* J. Stephen Jeans, "Waterways and Water Transportation," p. viii.

CHAPTER IV.

WATERWAYS AND RAILROADS AS CARRIERS.

From the foregoing account of the present condition of inland waterways of England and the United States it would hardly be expected that they, at least the canals, are capable of performing any very important commercial service. When one comes, however, to look into the actual tonnage of the freight moved on them the figures are found to be by no means small. The results of the investigation are encouraging; of course, the traffic on the important natural waterways is much greater than on any canals, but even the latter, when well located and constructed, show a large volume of freight. The object of this chapter is to inquire what are the actual services rendered by the railroads, the natural waterways and canals as carriers of freight.

The statistics of traffic on railroads is quite complete in all countries, but information concerning inland navigation is, with the exception of France, less thoroughly gathered. The statistics that are collected differ in character in each country, and do not furnish data for much instructive comparison of one country with another. In Germany the freight landed and loaded at each inland harbor and that which passes the port are noted; England leaves to the owners of waterways the collection of statistics in the way they choose. In the United States there had been no systematic attempt prior to the last census to collect any information concerning the traffic on inland waterways; and now the statistics, that we have, give but little data concerning inland navigation other than that on the Great Lakes and the Erie Canal, and on the rivers of the Mississippi Valley. No figures concerning the traffic on canals are given by the census, and in the case of seaport towns no distinction is made between inland and coastwise commerce. The statistics given are concerning all classes of transportation in the various ports of the United, States the figures being given separately for each of the five geographical divisions, the Atlantic Coast, Gulf of Mexico, Pacific Coast, Great Lakes and Mississippi Valley.* There is no division of freight into different classes of goods made in the census, except in the case of the Great Lakes and the Mississippi River and its tributaries. In both cases the freight is classified in four groups : products of agriculture, products of mines and quarries, other products, and, fourth, manufactures, miscellaneous merchandise and other commodities.

This diversity among nations as to the manner of collecting statistics of inland navigation, and classifying the freight moved on waterways led the Third International Congress on Inland Navigation, 1888, to appoint a committee to report on the best method of gathering and classifying these statistics. The committee reported to the Fourth International Congress, 1890, a detailed plan to be submitted to the several countries for adoption. As yet, however, no government has made any movement to secure similarity of statistics in different countries regarding inland navigation.

The kinds of freight adapted to carriage by water are, in general, the raw mining and agricultural products, and bulky manufactured articles of comparatively small value. Water transportation must, except in the case of certain large rivers

* The importance of our traffic by water, coastwise and on inland rivers, is worth noting. The following table is taken from the census, and is a "Statement showing the freight movement in tons by all classes of commercial craft of the United States operated during the year ending December 31, 1889:"

Geographical divisions.	Total all craft.	By steamers.	Sailing vessels.	Unrigged craft.
Totals	172,110,423	66,502,718	61,707,702	43,900,003
Atlantic Coast...........	77,597,626	28,778,341	38,283,401	10,535,884
Gulf of Mexico.........	2,864,956	1,455,450	1,359,526	49,980
Pacific Coast.............	8,818,363	5,741,940	2,761,826	314,597
Mississippi Valley.....	29,405,046	10,345,504		19,059,542
Great Lakes...............	53,424,432	20,181,483	19,302,949	13,940,000

and lakes, be slow, and when goods require speedy delivery either on account of their high value or their perishable nature they must be shipped by rail. Concerning the use of canals the Belgian Engineer, Theophile Finet, lays down the rule that, "To the canals must fall, as far as possible, the transportation of our raw materials, the railroads must handle everywhere the finished products, . . . all express, and all small articles of freight that are shipped in large quantities."* The line of separation cannot, however, be drawn so closely as this; the raw materials must exist in large quantities in order for the waterway to transport them to an advantage, and many finished products of a bulky character are well adapted to water transportation. The kinds of freight that seek transportation on large rivers and lakes where higher speed, larger cargoes and greater punctuality are possible, will differ from those going to canals. The dividing line between water and rail freights will be less rigidly drawn. In general it may be said that, other things being equal, goods will be shipped in the way most economical to industry; but even this truth must not be taken absolutely. Custom and conservatism are not without influence, and competition, foreign and domestic, is often required to induce men to employ the best and cheapest methods of manufacturing and transporting goods. Furthermore, whether or not shippers decide to send goods on either canals or natural waterways, instead of by rail, or *vice versa*, depends not only on the nature of the articles, but also on the circumstances connected with their shipment, and it cannot be said absolutely and categorically this kind of goods will go by water and that kind by rail. Coal, iron ore and wood, for instance, articles which generally admit of slower transportation, may under certain conditions demand more rapid movement. Again during some parts of the year the liability of accidents to freight sent by water may induce

* Stahl, "*Brennende Fragen Zum Bau und Bètrieb der Wasserstrassen*," pp. 169 and 181.

shippers to prefer the railroad. Most of all, if it be necessary to tranship goods in order to send them by water, merchants will frequently send them by rail at a higher rate. The first of these three circumstances influences the shipment of goods between places directly connected by rail or water, the third one conditions the choice of a railroad or waterway when sending by water necessitates a transhipment to another waterway or to a railroad.

Keeping these limitations in mind, it may be said that the freight that is actually shipped on waterways will indicate clearly enough the kinds of goods best adapted to water transportation. In each case it will be seen that bulky raw materials constitute the larger share; the kinds of raw materials depending on the industrial character of the region about the waterway. Of the tonnage on the Great Lakes in 1889, 27.96 per cent was iron ore, 24.97 per cent lumber, 22.24 per cent coal, and 12.39 per cent grain, these four articles thus comprising 87.56 per cent of all the freight. The Ohio, the Rhine and the Elbe may be taken as typical improved rivers. Out of a total of 5,528,857 tons shipped in 1889 on the Ohio River above Cincinnati, 65,550 tons were salt, 176,877 tons clay, sand and stone, 617,493 tons forest products, and 4,338,421 tons were coal. The freight forwarded from the ports of the Rhine is mostly coal, that being 72.26 per cent; wood constitutes 3.83 per cent, iron ore, 4.06 per cent; salt, about 1½ per cent; hewed stone and brick nearly the same share. The traffic on the Elbe up stream from Hamburg consists of a quite different class of raw materials. In 1889, 31 per cent was grain, 10 per cent manure, 9 per cent ores and metals, 5 per cent petroleum, and coal and wood each about 4 per cent. The character of canal freight is shown by shipments on the Erie Canal, of which the products of the farm, the forest and the mine constitute 76 per cent. The freight on the waterways at Berlin is mostly a barge traffic and affords a good example of inland navigation on ways practically artificial. Of the freight brought to Berlin in 1890, 49 per cent consisted of stone and brick, 21 per cent of lime, earth, sand, etc., 10 per cent of wood, 7 per cent of coal, and 6 per cent of grain.

Such is the nature of freight on inland waterways. What its amount is and how it compares with that of the railroads may be shown by a few statistics of the inland navigation of some of the leading countries. The traffic on the waterways of England was given in the previous chapter.

The statistics of the inland navigation in France are the most complete of those of any country. France is doing more than any other nation to improve her inland waterways, and their present condition may well be considered in this connection. By the law of the fifth of August, 1879, the navigable waterways were divided into two classes, principal and secondary, and the work of extending the principal ones and enlarging them to a common size which would permit the navigation of boats of three hundred tons burden was begun. The dimensions fixed upon were: Depth of water, 6 feet 7 inches; useful width of the locks, 17 feet; length of locks, 127 feet; clear height under the bridges, 11 feet 7 inches.

The length of the navigable rivers in France in 1880 was 6590 kilometres and of canals 4350 kilometres, the total length of both being 10,940 kilometres. The gain during the succeeding ten years was rapid. The lengths in 1890 were: Rivers, 7563 kilometres; canals, 4809 kilometres; total, 12,372 kilometres.

The "principal" waterways having the dimensions fixed by the law of 1879 were 1459 kilometres long in 1878, and 3965 kilometres in 1890. Of the 2506 kilometres increase, 1568 kilometres fell to the canals and 938 kilometres to the rivers. (Since 1880 the waterways of France have been free of tolls, and this together with the improvements made has caused a rapid increase in inland navigation) The amount and nature of the traffic on the French waterways in 1890 is shown by the following table:

Name of group	Tonnage		Total tonnage	Per cent of total traffic	Kilometre tons	Per cent of total k. tons	Mean dist. carried
	Rivers	Canals					
Mineral fuel	1,993,095	4,951,969	6,945,064	28.7	1,267,355,791	39.5	182
Building materials, minerals	4,212,248	3,475,348	7,687,596	31.8	531,800,150	16.6	69
Fertilizers	843,165	501,868	1,345,033	5.7	79,043,978	2.4	50
Wood	551,816	1,048,971	1,600,787	6.6	245,487,792	7.6	153
Machinery	19,888	4,750	24,638	0.1	4,326,047	0.1	175
Metals	424,803	1,288,653	1,713,456	7.1	373,283,415	11.6	218
Manufactures	288,125	390,246	678,371	2.8	155,208,281	4.8	243
Agricultural products	1,711,312	1,803,208	3,514,520	14.5	483,411,301	15.1	137
Sundries	134,376	211,280	345,656	1.4	39,558,515	1.2	114
Rafts	215,558	96,664	312,222	1.3	36,598,064	1.1	117
Total	10,394,386	13,772,957	24,167,343	100.00	3,216,073,334	100.00	133

As compared with 1881, the tonnage of 1890 shows an increase from 19,740,239 tons to 24,167,343 tons, or a gain of 22.4 per cent; but as the mean distance traveled by one ton increased from 110 to 133 kilometres, the kilometre tonnage rose from 2,174,531,107 tons kilometre in 1881 to 3,216,073,334 tons kilometre in 1890; that is, increased 47.8 per cent. It is a fact worthy of note that, as the above table shows, the canal traffic of France exceeds that on the rivers.

A comparison of the tonnage of the railroads of France with that of the waterways reveals some interesting facts: The kilometric tonnage of the railroads of France in 1890 was 11,759,084,088 tons kilometre, and that of the waterways 3,216,073,334. In 1881 the figures were respectively 10,752,834,568 and 2,174,531,107. Thus the railroads show an increase of only 9.3 per cent in ten years, or less than one per cent per annum; while the waterways, as indicated above, have increased their tonnage 47.8 per cent, or about 4.8 per cent a year. This fact is, of course, largely to be accounted for by the special favors which the French waterways have received during the decade.

If the total freight carried on waterways be compared with the total amount of like freight transported by rail it will be seen that the waterways carried in 1890 less than one-fourth

(23.84 per cent) of the total for both ways, the tonnage being 24,168,000 for the waterways, and, according to M. Fleury, of Paris, 79,180,000 for railroads. Not too much significance as to the commercial importance of waterways is to be attached to this fact. The territory served by the waterway is much less than that which makes use of the railroads. The railroads and waterways are not competitors for all traffic, and, again, only a part of the French waterways are so located that they may rightly be classed as principal, and of these only portions have been reconstructed and given the dimensions provided for by the law of 1879. The most fruitful comparison that could be made is between these larger reconstructed waterways and the railroads running parallel with them, but unfortunately the necessary data for this are not at hand. There were, in fact, in 1890 only 5621 kilometres of waterways and 4956 kilometres of railroads running parallel with each other in France,* and the length of the waterways having the dimensions provided for by the law of 1879— depth 6 feet 7 inches, width of locks 17 feet, length of lock 127 feet, height under bridges 11 feet 7 inches—was only 3288 kilometres.

The different waterways, even of France, present such a variety of dimensions as to hinder inland navigation. The necessity for having common dimensions for waterways and their locks must be apparent to all. Suppose that the railroads connecting Chicago and New York consisted of five parts each with different dimensions so that freight between the two places would have to be transhipped four times, what would be the effect on transportation by rail! The tonnage would be much smaller and the ton mileage would fall proportionally more than the tonnage. The influence of giving a part of the French waterways like-dimensions has been to increase both the volume of traffic and its average distance of shipment.

* *Cf.* Fleury, pp. 18-19. "Report on Respective Uses of Waterways and Railways," to the Fifth International Congress on Inland Navigation.

The traffic on German waterways is large, chiefly because of the long navigable rivers of the country. The Rhine, Weser, Elbe and Oder are important streams flowing from the forests and mines of the South through the agricultural plains of the North to the large seaports on the Baltic and North Seas. These conditions, most favorable to commerce, have been turned to good account by the improvement of the rivers, and now there is on the Rhine and Elbe and lower Oder a large and important traffic. The shipments at the German ports of the Rhine reached 13,151,246 tons in 1890. The total for all the Rhine was 18,971,072 tons.* The navigable length of the German portion of the Rhine is about the same as the main line of the Reading Railroad, and it is an interesting fact that the traffic on the two is about the same. The total tonnage on the Elbe in 1890 was about 8,000,000 tons. The passenger traffic on these rivers is naturally important, though the figures when compared with those for the railroads seem small. The two more important of the three companies running passenger steamers on the Rhine carried 1,172,354 persons in 1890. The same year 2,348,000 persons made use of the Elbe in Saxony and Bohemia; this passenger traffic, however, was more local than that of the Rhine.

The connection of these large rivers by means of canals has been only partially accomplished. Three short canals in Brandenburg enable the traffic of the Elbe and Oder to reach Berlin. Over four million tons of freight, exclusive of rafts, were taken by boat to Berlin in 1890, nearly as much as was brought to the city by all the railroads.† The other canals of Germany have only a small traffic, either because of their poor location, or by reason of their small dissimilar dimensions. Prussia is now constructing a canal from the coal mines at

* In reality the amount is more than this, statistics being collected at only the principal ports, much that is shipped is not counted. One basalt company, for instance, shipped 414,856 tons of which no account was made in the statistics.

† This shows the possibilities of barge traffic to-day, even under only moderately favorable conditions. The average lading of a boat was only 114 tons.

Dortmund to the seaport Emden, and has authorized a Rhine-Elbe canal to connect the Rhine region with the Elbe and Oder and thus the mining West with the agricultural East. Prussia and the Empire are together constructing the Nord-Ost-see Canal to join the German Ocean with the Baltic Sea by means of a waterway through German Territory. These works, when completed, will surely greatly increase the inland navigation of Germany. Because of the method of collecting statistics only of the freight loaded and unloaded at the principal ports, the actual traffic at present cannot be accurately stated. In 1885 these statistics for 8900 kilometres of waterways showed a kilometric tonnage, exclusive of the coast-wise commerce, of 3,535,000,000, and it is estimated that the traffic, concerning which statistics are lacking, would bring the total up to 4,800,000,000 tons kilometre for all German waterways.*

The relation between the traffic by rail and by water in Germany acquires added interest from the fact that the State owns both means of transportation. The railroads and waterways being under separate management, however, not a little rivalry has existed between the two ways and this has tended to hinder the best co-ordination of the railroads and waterways. This has of late been less evident, the mutual relationship of the two agents has been more friendly, and the commerce by water has relatively increased. In 1890 thirty per cent of the inland traffic of Germany moved by water. The equality of shipments to Berlin by rail and on waterways essentially artificial has been mentioned. The uselessness of setting over against the 100,918,874 tons of freight moved, 1890, by all the railroads of the German portion of the Rhine Valley the 13,714,372 tons carried on the Rhine must be self-evident. To do this is to compare the traffic of 6800 miles of railways, consisting of twenty lines starting from a great many cities and radiating in all directions to supply the markets of the interior and the most

* *Cf.* Schlichting, Conrad's *Handworterbuch*, Vol. ii., p. 837.

distant parts of the Empire with goods of all descriptions, with the freight moved on the 1172 miles of the waterways, rivers and canals, of the Rhine Valley, that is, with but a few water routes and those practically without water communication with other parts of Germany, water routes whose tonnage is from the nature of the case composed of fewer articles of transportation than the railroads carry. Indeed, the German Rhine, constituting less than a third of the total 1172 miles of the navigable waterways of the German Rhine Valley, is the only part adapted to the needs of present navigation. We find, for instance, that nine-tenths of the coal—the article especially fitted to water transportation—that is shipped in the Rhine Valley goes by rail and one-tenth by water; but if the coal shipments from Duisburg, Ruhrort, and Hochfeld, Rhine ports of the Westphalian coal region, be examined, it is found that the railroads carry only forty per cent as much as the Rhine.* In general, it may be said that the traffic on the German waterways is large and is increasing *pari passu* with that of the railroads; when the work of further connecting the separated systems of natural waterways is completed the freight on the waterways will assume much larger proportions than it now possesses.

Definite statistical comparison of the traffic by rail and by water within the United States is even more difficult than in the case of other countries. With the exception of the Erie Canal we know very little about the tonnage of goods moved on canals, and to contrast freight movements on parallel railroads and rivers is practically impossible. The immense proportions of our inland commerce both by rail and by water are familiar facts. Our most important barge canal is the Erie which is used to transport three to three and a half million tons yearly. The eleventh census gives detailed statistics concerning the traffic on the rivers of the Mississippi System. The facts of the Ohio River and its branches, above Cincinnati,

---

* *Cf.* Van der Borght, p. 7, Report to the Fifth International Congress on Inland Navigation.

WATERWAYS AND RAILROADS AS CARRIERS. 47

are especially interesting; here 5214 craft in 1889 moved 10,744,063 tons of freight. The ton mileage was 2,076,866,-145 ton miles, each ton being moved on an average nearly two hundred miles. The figures quite warrant the statement in the census "that the waterways of the Ohio River and its tributaries are, under present conditions of transportation, of great importance so far as low-class freight is concerned." The tonnage of the rivers of the Mississippi Valley, 1890, was placed at 31,050,058 tons; this, though large, is probably less than the actual amount. To move this freight and to carry the 10,858,894 passengers that made use of the river, 7445 boats were employed. The commerce on the Great Lakes is enormous. The total tonnage passing the St. Mary's lock, between Lake Superior and Lake Huron, was, for the year ending June 30, 1892, 10,107,603 tons. The ton mileage of the lake freight in 1890 was 18,849,681,384 ton miles, 27½ per cent of the ton mileage of all the railroads of the United States.

There is no necessity for multiplying statistics of this kind. The magnitude and importance of the commerce of our large inland lakes and rivers are well-known. The present traffic on the canals in the United States is small and for reasons which have been sufficiently elaborated. We know very little about the use that is actually made of most of our canals now in operation, and if we did the information would be of little significance as regards the real relation of artificial waterways, equipped with the most modern improvements, to railways as carriers of freight. It is useless to compare the canal as it now is to the railroad. Were we to compare an ox and a horse as to the services each can perform, we should doubtless agree that the horse moves quicker and is able to do more kinds of work; but justice to the ox would compel us to take animals of equal age and soundness. So with the canal.

CHAPTER V.

INFLUENCE OF INLAND WATER ROUTES ON RAILROAD TARIFFS.

The influence of canals, improved rivers and lakes, as regulators of railroad tariffs, is a subject of interest alike to those countries whose railways are under private ownership and management and to those which themselves own the means of transportation. The control of rates on private railroads has presented to legislators a problem they have as yet been able only partially to solve. After sixty years of effort on the part of the English Parliament, first to prevent combination, then to secure reasonable rates, England has the highest railway charges of any country. The establishment of maximum rates by law is no guarantee of moderate charges. In this country the attempt to control rates by rail led to the vigorous attack of the Western States against the railroads by means of the "Granger legislation." This policy was soon abandoned, and the State railroad commissions were given wider powers and increased functions. The State commissions having no power to lay down rules concerning charges on interstate commerce, the national commission was established in 1886 with power to supervise interstate traffic, and to compel revisions of rates when charges are unreasonable or when they are unfair to particular shippers. All this is evidence that some control over the administration of private railway companies and some regulation of their tariffs are considered necessary. The results of the commissions' efforts, whatever may be said of their value, and they are indeed important, have in no sense solved the question of rate charges. Only the threshold of the problem has been reached, and the investigations of the commission have only enforced the need and importance of inland waterways to set limits to railroad charges and to exercise a constant pressure in the direction of cheaper rates and more efficient service.

There is a vital difference between the railway and the public waterway. The lakes and large navigable rivers of every country are public highways accessible to all. Any shipper who will may navigate them with his own boats, and at present usually without payment. Canals owned by the State are likewise highways, either free or toll, and those owned by corporations or individuals are usually, at least in theory, ways on which individual shippers may compete. With the railway it is different; the conditions necessary to its successful management have, at least up to the present, prevented its being a highway open to the common use of individual shippers. As is well known, the railroad was at first supposed to be of the same character as the turnpike. The first laws both in England and in the American States were framed with that idea in mind. It was not long before the error was discovered, and in 1839 the fact of the inability of individual shippers to compete on a railroad by running their own cars and trains was definitely recognized by Parliament.

Another truth, and one of greater significance, began to manifest itself early in the history of railroads, viz., the fact that *combination and monopoly, and not competition, is the natural law governing the relations of railways to each other.* This law was not so easily comprehended as was the fact of the difference between the railway and the turnpike; indeed, there are still many to-day who fail to comprehend the monopolistic character of railroad business. It may be said, as a general statement, that the chief aim of legislation for the control of railway charges has been to maintain competition in a business which is by nature monopolistic.

A few persons early discovered the real nature of the railway. As early as 1836, Mr. Morrison, a man whose voice on later occasions was often heard on railroad questions, made a speech in Parliament that can be read with profit:

even to-day.* "Suppose," he said, "that, in spite of all the difficulties opposed to the formation of a new company, one is formed, obtains an act, and actually comes into competition with the present line, would not the obvious interests of both parties, unless prevented by such precaution as I have proposed (periodical revision of rates by the government), inevitably bring about some understanding between them by which the high charges would be further confirmed and all chances of competition removed to a greater distance."†

The inefficiency of competition between railroads to regulate tariffs and insure reasonable rates was clearly emphasized by Mr. Gladstone in 1844 in his speech in support of the railway bill of that year to provide a modicum of parliamentary control of railroads. "It was said let matters go on as at present, and let the country trust to the effects of competition. Now for his part he would rather give his confidence to a Gracchus, when speaking on the subject of sedition, than give his confidence to a railway director, speaking to the public of the effect of competition—railway companies were singularly philanthropic among themselves. Their quarrels were like lovers' quarrels and they reminded him of a quotation once felicitously made use of by Mr. Fox : '*Breves inimicitiæ, amicitiæ sempiturnæ.*' "‡

* Hansard's Parliamentary Debates, third series, vol. xxxiii., p. 980.

† The advocates of the municipal ownership of water, gas, electric lighting, etc., will be interested in one of the arguments used by Mr. Morrison to substantiate his thesis. "The history of our metropolitan water companies is most instructive on this point. After a fierce contention among themselves, they came to an agreement by which they parceled the town into districts; and having assigned one to each company, they left it to obtain from the inhabitants the utmost it can obtain, and to profit, without let or hindrance of any kind, by the extension of this ever-growing metropolis! The public, too, is served not merely with a dear, but also a bad article; and the probability of relief is more distant than it would have been had some of the companies not been established."

It is interesting to compare this statement, made in 1836, with one made in 1893, concerning the electric lighting company of Philadelphia: "At present the compactly built areas are parceled out among existing companies by an agency which refuses to declare itself except in its actions. The monopoly thus established possesses such power over Councils that the city will be forced to expend about $225,000 in 1893 in excess of the amount for which it could produce the light," etc. Report of the Citizens' Municipal Association of Philadelphia.

‡ Hansard's Debates, third series, vol. lxxvi., p. 500.

WATER ROUTES AND RAILROAD TARIFFS. 51

The tendency toward combination is equally strong in the case of railroads and competing private waterways, and unless prevented from so doing they will unite to secure higher rates. In England this was observed by Parliament to be the case as early as 1840, and the subsequent struggle of the two agents of commerce furnished ample evidence of the strength of the tendency. The English railroads usually bought the canals, because they wanted to control rates, and seldom because they wished to use the waterway for moving freight. The chief purpose of English legislation, since 1872, has been to stop the destruction of the canals by the railroads, and, by keeping the waterways independent, to preserve them as regulators of freight tariffs.

In America, as well as in England, it was early attempted to prevent the combination of waterways with railroads and to preserve the former as regulators of the charges by the latter. Article XVII ; Section 4 of the Constitution, which Pennsylvania adopted in 1873, declares :

"No railroad, canal, or other corporation, or the lessees, purchasers or managers of any railroad or canal corporation, shall consolidate the stock, property, or franchises of such corporation, with, or lease or purchase the works or franchises of, or in any way control any other railroad or canal corporation owning, or having under its control a parallel or competing line ; nor shall any officer of such railroad or canal corporation act as an officer of any other railroad or canal corporation owning or having the control of a parallel or competing line ; and the question whether railroads or canals are parallel or competing lines: shall, when demanded by the party complainant, be decided by a jury, as in other civil issues."

That the American legislation availed even less than the English in checking the consolidation of railroads with one another or with canals was made evident by the discussion in the preceding chapter on the present condition of English and American waterways. In America we have not been so assiduous as have the English in trying to control rates by endeavoring to check the workings of the law of consolidation and monopolization in the railway business. A bill, for instance, introduced this year into the Pennsylvania Senate to enforce the above clause of the Constitution was reported with a negative recommendation. But if we had tried as hard as England we should doubtless have had no greater success than she.

Competition, it is true, is not absent from the railroad business. It is felt in many instances in through freight and passenger traffic between important and distant centres, and has been the spur that has urged forward many improvements in service, and kept down freight rates to numerous shipping points. Competition has even been strong enough, it will be said, to lead to many railroad wars. An analysis of competition between railroads, however, shows it to exist at only comparatively few points. Moreover, when and where it has obtained strongly, and has led to war, its working has been spasmodic and harmful rather than beneficial. The railway war is usually followed, as are other wars, by increased taxes to cover the costs of the conflict.

There is every effort made by railway managers to avoid competition one with another. The few important systems are rapidly getting control of the principal lines of the United States, and they are following up this action by one that naturally succeeds. They are dividing up the country into sections, each system receiving control of the traffic of a special portion. As one instance out of many may be cited the action taken last March by the "New York, New Haven and Hartford Railroad" and the "Boston and Maine." A joint committee represented on the part of the New Haven by J. Pierpont Morgan, William Rockefeller and William D. Bishop, and on the part of the Boston and Maine by Frank Jones, G. G. Haven and Samuel C. Lawrence, met and agreed to divide New England between the two roads. Their agreement was ratified by the directors of the two companies, and was to the effect that the Boston and Maine should have that part of New England north of the "Boston and Albany" line, and that the New Haven should have the portion south of that. Each company agreed not to interfere with the territory of the other and to interchange, as far as possible, all the business of the two territories.

There is a growing dissatisfaction with competition between railroads as the safeguard of the public's interests, and a growing conviction that combinations and pooling agreements are for the good of the public as well as the railroads. Railroad managers are, it is true, in favor of combination and pooling, and there is no doubt that their concern is rather for their own dividends than for the weal of the public; but up to a certain limit—which limit we must look to governmental control to find and establish in such a way as to prevent its being overstepped by the railways—the interests of the railroads and the public are common. The Interstate Commerce Commission, to whom the American people look as one means of defending their interests against the encroachments of the railroads, favor pooling, and rightly believe that regulated combination is more to be desired than attempts to keep up a competition among railroads.* A uniform classification of freight common to all roads, stability of rates, and equal treatment, under similar conditions, of all shippers by carriers are the main objects that the commission is striving to attain. Believing that stability of rates and prevention of discriminations are impossible without allowing pooling contracts, it caused a bill to be introduced into the Senate in December, 1892, permitting contracts between competing lines for the division of freight, subject to the approval or disapproval of the Interstate Commerce Commission. Of course the desirability of permitting pooling is a question on which there is difference of opinion. The bill to permit pooling failed to

* "The railroads of this country are practically parts of one great system instead of being, as is popularly supposed, made up of individual lines, each having the right to act independently of the others. For the prevention of this waste of strife, as well as contributing to equality of service, that form of traffic compacts called a pool agreement promises to afford the desired relief, by removing from carriers the possibility of profiting either individually or collectively by such means." James Peabody, editor of the *Railway Review*, on "The Necessity for Railway Compacts under Governmental Regulation," in the *Independent*, June 1, 1893.

reach the Senate. The chairman of the Committee on Interstate Commerce, Mr. Cullom, and the majority of his associates were opposed to the bill and their attitude was made less friendly by the fact that the chief advocates of the measure were railroad presidents.

Still time must surely show that the Senate committee was in error and demonstrate the correctness of the position taken by the Interstate Commerce Commission. That pooling alone will secure low rates is not the contention, but history plainly shows that the principle of combination, to enforce which pooling is a device, is being recognized as the dominant one. Attempts to maintain competition by the prevention of pooling will, in the long run, be futile,* and were it possible for them to succeed they would not ultimately secure as cheap rates as combination under government regulation; they would establish in the railroad business a law antagonistic to its most efficient and most economical management.†

The best regulator of railroad rates is the independent waterway. Competition between railroads and water routes is quite different in kind from that of railroads with each other; it is bound to produce cheaper rates, and can do this without detriment to the railroads. The present chapter will show how extensive and important a power the waterway exerts in lowering charges by rail; the influence of this on the railroads will be discussed in the next chapter.

There is abundant evidence showing the power of water transportation to lower freight rates. The past and present opposition which the railroads have shown the waterways in

---

* Witness the agreement of last November (1892) among the trunk lines in regard to passenger rates to the World's Fair.

† By a resolution of the Senate, April 15, 1893, the Senate Committee on Interstate Commerce has been empowered to carry on an investigation concerning certain alleged weaknesses of the law regulating interstate commerce, with a view to proposing amendments. The resolution enumerates the following four subjects for the committee to investigate: pooling, the short haul clause, Canadian competition, and labor on railroads. Of course the committee can introduce amendments on as many other subjects as it may see fit.

order that rates might be controlled indicates clearly enough that the railroads are conscious of the potency of water competition. The railroads see in the waterway an agency which can move certain kinds of freight at lower rates than they can be transported on land; and without analyzing the results of this to see what may be the secondary effects on the freight business by rail of the cheaper transportation charges for these certain kinds of goods, the railroad strives to quash the waterway out of existence. The success of the railroad companies of England, of Pennsylvania and of Ohio in this regard has been noted.

An illustration out of many that might be cited to show the real and effective competition of waterways is afforded by Belgium.* Liége and Antwerp are connected by a line of navigation 156 kilometres long that comes in competition with two railroads somewhat shorter in length. The water rates "often come as low as" 2 francs 15 centimes to 2 francs 30 centimes per ton for the entire distance. In order to compete, the railroads carry at their lowest rate between Liége and Antwerp. In train load lots of 200 tons, for exportation by sea, they charge only two francs a ton. This is a special rate, all others being enough higher than by boat to enable the waterways to secure a good volume of freight.

The cheapest freight rates by rail to be found in the world are those for grain between Chicago and New York; and why? Because the cheapest inland water transportation rates in the world are those between the same points. All the railroads of the United States have been steadily lowering freight charges during the past twenty years, and largely, of course, because improvements in track and equipment have made this possible. Those roads, however, that have made the most improvements and the greatest reductions in rates are the great trunk lines leading into New York from the West, those that compete with the Great Lakes, the Erie Canal and

* Dufourny, p. 9 of article in Report of Fourth International Congress on Inland Navigation.

the Hudson River. The average freight earnings per ton mile of all the railroads of the United States for the year ending June 30, 1890, were .941 cents.* The ton mile earnings of the New York Central and Hudson River Railroad were .730 cents, and on the Pennsylvania Railroad, .661 cents; on the Lake Shore and Michigan Southern, .653 cents, and on the Michigan Central, .726 cents; whereas the average earnings per ton mile on the Chicago, Milwaukee and St. Paul, and the Chicago and Northwestern, roads coming but slightly into competition with the Great Lakes and other waterways, were 1.06 and 1.03 cents respectively. The following table,† showing the wheat rates per bushel from Chicago to New York for the years 1870, 1880 and 1889, by water, by water and rail combined, and by rail, indicates very plainly how freight rates have fallen and how this movement has been led by the waterways:

	By lake and canal.	By lake and rail.	By all rail.
1870 . . .	17.10 cents.	22.0 cents.	33.3 cents.
1880 . . .	12.27 "	15.7 "	19.9 "
1889 . . .	6.89 "	8.7 "	15.0 "

The important influence of the Erie Canal on freight rates has often been emphasized; only a few facts need be given here. They are for the year 1891:

The Erie Canal was opened in May, at which time the pool rates on grain from Buffalo to New York were seven and four-fifths cents per bushel. The grain rates on the canal for the various months of the season were, May, 2.51 cents; June, 2.53 cents; July, 2.68 cents; August, 3.94 cents; September, 4.19 cents; October, 4.44 cents; and November, 4.13 cents. The railroad pool rates, though nominally unchanged, were not maintained. Mr. Edward Hannan,

*For the year ending June 30, 1891, they were .895 cents.
† See "Commercial Policy of the United States of America, 1860-1890," by Smith and Seligman.

Superintendent of Public Works of New York, says :* "My information on that subject, which has been received from private sources, is that contracts were made by the various railroads to carry grain in the months of June, July and August, for four cents a bushel ; September, four and one-half ; and October five cents."

On petition of the Merchants' Exchange, of Buffalo, the Superintendent of Public Works kept the canals of New York State open five days longer than the allotted time. This shows very plainly that shippers regard the canal as a freight regulator. When the canals closed for the winter, the railroad charges again rose to the pool rates.

Of course the Great Lakes and the Erie Canal, though very important, constitute only one of the waterways that compete with the railroads of the United States. On the Mississippi River and its numerous long branches there is an immense traffic setting limits not only to the charges on freight by rail carried up and down the valley, but also to a large extent on that carried out of the valley. The grain rates in 1888, from St. Louis to New York, changed from ten cents a bushel in September to twenty-nine cents during December and January, when the Mississippi River was closed to traffic.†

These great natural waterways exercise the most important influence of any of the inland navigable routes of the United States on the charges which railroads make ; but the smaller streams are not without their effect. Whenever the improvement of a stream has given shippers a choice of means of transportation, the freight rates on the articles having such option have been cheapened.

One of the questions which the Senate [Cullom] Committee on Interstate Commerce sent out in 1885 when making the investigation which preceded the framing of the bill establishing the Interstate Commerce Commission was : "In

* See his Report on canals of the State, 1891, page 20.
† *Cf.* Sering. p. 505. "*Die landwirtschaftliche Konkurrenz Nord-americas in Gegenwart und Zukunft.*"

making provision for securing cheap transportation, is it or is it not important that the government should develop and maintain a system of water routes?" The answers to the question, and the testimony before the committee embodied the views of ninety men, most of whom were eminent in railroading and the transportation business; and seventy-three out of ninety agreed in regarding "a national system of internal water communication as the most certain and effective method of regulating railroad rates and of insuring to the people the advantages of cheap transportation." *

The total volume of freight by rail within the United States and every other country is, of course, much larger than that by water. The reasons why this is now so, and will continue to be so, were noted in discussing the traffic in the Rhine Valley. The waterways, however, can regulate rates by carrying only a fraction as much as the competing railroad; and it by no means proves the inability of the waterway to fix rates to show that the volume of freight passing over the railroads is several times that on the competing routes of navigation. The rate charged by the waterway sets a limit—not so low, it is true, as the tariff on the waterway—beyond which the railroad cannot go without surrendering its traffic to the waterway. The traffic will bear only a much more limited rate by rail when transportation by water is possible.

A well-informed engineer, John L. Van Ornum, Chief Topographer of the International Boundary Survey which has just been made between the United States and Mexico, says: "It is the universal experience in America that water communication tends to keep down railway rates. Instances are not rare where railways have carried freight for the same rate that competing boats have done until the boats have been sent away or sold on account of lack of business, and then at once the railways have raised their tariffs. In all the number of instances I know of, when water navigation has been resumed, the competing railways have been obliged to

* See Senate Reports, 1st sess., 49th Cong. 1885-86, vol. ii., part 1, p. 2 of Appendix.

lower their rates. Herein lies the great value of our waterways, not so much in actual tonnage carried, as in their far-reaching indirect effect in forcing down railway rates."*

The influence of the waterway on tariffs is felt beyond the regions immediately bordering the navigable route. When, for instance, the Lakes, the Erie Canal and Hudson River fix the rail rates from Chicago to New York, they also fix the limits of charges from such interior cities as St. Louis, Indianapolis and Cincinnati to the East. The testimony before the Hepburn Committee was to the effect that by agreement of the roads existing at that time, the rate from Chicago to New York was taken as a basis and the charges on slow freight from Cincinnati, Kansas City, Louisville, etc., were made a certain percentage of that basis; such a percentage, that is to say, as would prevent freight from being sent first to a lake port and then shipped east by water instead of being forwarded directly through by rail.†

The influence of the Great Lakes on rates is shown by the following illustration: For certain reasons, rates on coal from the East are cheaper to Duluth than to Chicago; and thus, it comes about, that Duluth dealers can sell coal as far south as Kansas City, and supply many cities that are much nearer Chicago. As another illustration may be mentioned, the case of Aberdeen, Watertown, Huron, and other Dakota cities, where wheat rose seven cents a bushel and coal fell two dollars a ton, when railway connections with Lake Superior were secured.

The influence of waterways on tariffs by rail must increase and widen with the future growth of unity in freight classifications and charges. The Interstate Commerce Commission, recognizing the fact, that uniformity of freight classifications among different companies is necessary to any effective

---

* Quoted from a letter written January, 1892.

† It is not at present necessary to elaborate this well-known idea of Albert Fink. His testimony before the Hepburn Committee, however, attributes to waterways a greater influence on railroad charges at the present time than I should admit.

governmental regulation of freight charges, has vigorously labored to induce railroads to adopt a uniform classification. The roads north of the Ohio and east of the Mississippi have generally adopted the classification recommended by the National Commission; those of the West have worked out another one more especially fitted to the condition of the territory which they serve. The movement is toward complete uniformity throughout the United States; indeed, the American people will, before long, insist, not only that there be a uniform classification, but also, that the charges made by the railroad companies shall be fixed throughout their respective lines according to a definite system, and that rates shall be given fullest publicity. When this state of affairs comes to exist, the influence of water competition must surely be still more far-reaching. The principle of fixing rates, to which Albert Fink alludes, will in the future have far wider application than it has at present.

As the improvement and co-ordination of the inland waterways of the United States continues, their control of freight rates will increase. When the projected improvements of the Great Lakes and the Mississippi River shall have been completed, and these systems of waterways shall have been connected with each other and with the Atlantic Ocean by canals of adequate dimensions, when the Columbia River and other streams of the Pacific Slope shall have been improved and the West joined to the East by means of the Nicaragua Canal, then for the first time will the real significance of our inland waterways as regulators of freight charges be manifest.

No one, it is to be hoped, will interpret the foregoing discussion to imply that the small, ill-equipped, antiquated canals constructed three-quarters of a century ago, to meet the requirements of the commerce of that time, can exert any important control over railroad traffic. The waterways which have such power are those that more or less fully meet the requirement of the commerce of to-day.

WATER ROUTES AND RAILROAD TARIFFS. 61

Furthermore, in order for inland waterways to control the charges on private railways, they must be independent of the ownership or control of the railroads. From the description of the English canals that was given in Chapter III., it is not to be expected that the freight rates by rail in that country are much influenced by the waterways. There is, in fact, but little competition, and the result of this is a very high rate of charges. The average ton mile rate on the railways of the United Kingdom for heavy traffic is nearly double the average freight earnings of the railways of the United States. This difference is to be accounted for partly by the existence in the United States of great masses of raw products, which are carried long distances; but more by the fact that a large part of these products may be carried either by water or by rail.

The conclusion to which the Cullom Committee came as the result of its investigation in 1885 on the effect of water competition upon railroad charges is in perfect harmony with the position taken in this discussion. The report to the Senate was that, "the evidence before the committee accords with the experience of all nations in recognizing the water routes as the most efficient cheapeners and regulators of railway charges. Their influence is not confined within the limits of the territory immediately accessible to water communication, but extends further, and controls railroad rates at such remote and interior points as have competing lines reaching means of transport by water. Competition between railroads sooner or later leads to combination or consolidation, but neither can prevail to secure unreasonable rates in the face of direct competition with free natural or artificial water routes. The conclusion of the committee is, therefore, that natural or artificial channels of communication by water, when favorably located, adequately improved, and properly maintained, afford the cheapest method of long distance transportation now known, and that they must continue to exercise in the future, as they have invariably exercised in the past, an absolutely controlling and beneficially regulating influence upon the charges made upon any and all means of transit."

It will be noticed that the discussions of this chapter have had in view the relation between waterways and private railroads. The treatment of the subject will not be complete until an analysis has been made of the influence of inland navigation on the rates that may and must be charged on State-owned railways; but as this part of the subject fits best into the chapter that is to follow, it may be postponed till the general influence of inland water transportation on railroad revenues has been considered.

CHAPTER VI.

INFLUENCE OF INLAND WATERWAYS ON RAILWAY REVENUES.

The relationship between waterways and railroads as freight carriers is but half expounded by showing that inland navigation is the most important regulator of the railroad charges for the transportation of several important categories of freight; it still remains to investigate the effect which this lowering of charges has on the net receipts of the railway companies. If net profits of the railroads are seriously cut into by the competition of waterways, the results can hardly avoid being injurious to the best development of the means of transportation and communication. Although it is doubtless true that in special cases the railroads, by means of monopolistic powers, secure an unduly high rate of gains; this can hardly be said of the railroad business in general. It would be unfortunate, both for the public and for the railroads, were the government or any other agency to inaugurate a policy that would lessen the returns on capital invested in railroads. It is to the interest of the public that railroad capital should return good profits, in order that railway companies may continue to pay their employés well for their work that the companies may be able to improve the service rendered the public and to extend their system of roads to every nook and corner of the country. The State can have no object in restricting the freest development of the railroad. The interests of passengers and shippers ought to be guarded by careful legislation, but to disregard the interests of the railways, in so doing, is to commit as grave an error as to neglect the the welfare of those who ship goods or travel by rail.

Water competition is not ruinous but helpful to the railroads. If waterways be extended and their regulative power over rail rates be increased they will prove no hindrance to the development of the railroads. This statement may seem somewhat paradoxical, but is, in fact, not at all so. The two means of communication are very different agents of commerce; they compete with each other for the carriage of several kinds of traffic, and with sufficient force to influence strongly the charges by rail; but *the waterway does more than compete; it both aids and complements the railroad.* This fact cannot be too strongly emphasized. It must be kept in mind throughout the consideration of the relation of waterways and railways. The two means of transportation do not perform the same work, but services that are largely distinct and complementary to each other.

Not all the freight transported by water would be moved by rail if the waterway did not exist. Canals, rivers and lakes create a large share of their traffic. The cost of transportation determines to a large extent the amount of goods shipped. Cheaper rates give to existing categories of freight a larger and wider market, and introduce into commerce new articles, such, for instance, as sand, stone, straw, fertilizers and wood, which were formerly unable to bear the costs of transportation. Again, the waterway creates traffic for the railroads as well as for itself. It makes raw materials cheaper, increases the number of those that are available for use, and thus adds to the products of agriculture and manufacture seeking transportation. The effects of increasing and cheapening raw materials are complex; cheaper wholesale and retail prices and higher wages are possible, and these in turn prepare the way for a larger and more varied consumption of goods. This means important additions to the shipments, especially of manufactured goods, the kind of freight which from its nature falls mainly to the railroads.

The statistics of the traffic of the railways and waterways at Frankfort-on-the-Main, before and after the canalization of the Main from Mayence to Frankfort, show in a striking way that an increase in water traffic may be accompanied by an equal or greater rise in the traffic of competing railroads.

The improvement of the Main from Mayence to Frankfort was completed at the close of 1886. The following table gives the tonnage by rail and by water for the three years before and for the three years succeeding the canalization of the Main.*

	Traffic on waterways and railways. Tons.	On the waterways. Tons.	Increase over previous year.	On the railways.	Increase over previous year.
1884	1,014,518.7	150,513.7		864,005	
1885	1,047,845.0	150,805.0	281.3	897,040	33,035
1886	1,088,046.8	155,956.8	5,151.8	932,090	35,050
Average of the 3 years.	1,050,136.8	152,425.2		897,712	
1887	1,373,690.8	360,062.8	204,106.0	1,013,628	81,538
1888	1,748,733.1	516,798.1	156,735.3	1,231,935	218,307
1889†	1,911,758.4	577,610.4	60,812.3	1,334,148	102,213

The table shows that the total increase of the tonnage of 1888 on that of the average for the years 1884–85–86 was 698,596 tons; by this increase the waterways gained 364,373 tons, and the railways 334,223 tons. The gain of 1889 on that of the average for the years 1884–85–86 was 861,621.6 tons; and in this instance the railways show greater gains than do the waterways. The waterways and railways increased their tonnage 425,185.2 and 436,436.4 tons respectively. The great gains in the tonnage of the railroad since the canalization of the Main as compared with the gains before is seen if the yearly increase be noted.

Was this increase in traffic due to other causes than the canalization of the Main, and could it have taken place without the waterway? If so, the entire increase in freight might have been secured by the railroads. According to Consul Puls of the Chamber of Commerce of Frankfort, the products of the interior, such as wood, loam and building materials, secured a greater market through the canalization

* Report of Fourth International Congress on Inland Navigation, p. 59.
† The relative decline in the increase of the tonnage both of waterways and railroads in 1889 was due to a strike. The increase of the railroads in 1890 was again large.

of the river. The industrial activity of Frankfort increased because of cheaper raw materials, especially coal. The amount of traffic from Frankfort to the sea was greatly enlarged, by rail and by water, and the railroads profited both by a growth in their freight and by an equalization in volumes carried up and down from the sea to Frankfort. This equalization was an advantage to the railroads, because it enabled them to run fewer empty wagons, and thus to reduce the expenses of operation.

An important consideration, and one that has not received due attention, is that much of the freight taken from the railroad for water transportation involves little or no real net loss to railway companies. Railroads, especially the American, are doing an immense amount of business which brings them little or no direct profit. Operating expenses constitute a large share—sixty-seven per cent—of earnings, and this is because a great deal of bulky freight is carried at a rate so low that the costs of operation often include ninety per cent of earnings. Indeed, it is asserted that coal, coke, stone and iron ore are sometimes carried at a loss by the railroads in order that by so doing they may keep down the prices of crude products and thus sustain industry and enlarge the volume of higher grades of traffic.* The operating expenses on the German railroads constitute only fifty-five per cent of the gross earnings. Were the American railways to give over a good share of their bulky freight to the waterways it would not materially reduce their net profits. Grain is another article of transportation on which the railroads make only small profits. Grain rates are much lower in America than in Germany, but local freight tariffs are much higher.† American railroads are making the local freights pay for the trouble of handling grain at low profit.

There are several advantages even which would flow to the railroads from the surrender of a large share of this

---

* *Cf.* Thomas P. Roberts, p. 10 of "Report on Waterways and Railways" to Fifth International Congress on Inland Navigation.

† *Cf.* Sering. "*Die landwirthschaftliche Konkurrenz Nord-americas.*"

bulky low-tariff freight. It would allow them to expand the volume of fast freight and increase passenger traffic and this, too, by means of a proportionally less outlay-of-capital.

The amount of travel in any country, even more than the volume of freight, is conditioned by rates, and is capable of almost indefinite expansion. The results of the zone tariff in Austria and Hungary * suggest in a small way how it is possible to add to travel by reducing rates. A great reduction in the local rates on the railroads that centre in London and other great cities, however, could not, under the present conditions, correspondingly increase the travel ; because of the inability of the railroads to handle the passengers. † The morning and evening trains are now crowded ; the number of trains that can be run is limited ; and only at a very great cost could the room for stations and yards be enlarged sufficiently to meet the requirements of a greatly increased travel. Some roads, as for instance the Pennsylvania within Philadelphia, actually discourage purely local traffic. The development of the waterways leading into London could relieve the railroads of the burden of much of their slow, bulky freight, enable them to clear their tracks for passenger trains, and allow them more track room for their passenger trains in the city and permit them to enlarge their terminal facilities for handling passengers.

The expansion not only of local but also of long distance passenger traffic depends upon freeing the railroads of some of its bulky freight. The trunk lines of the United States, are now over-crowded ; they refused to make a large reduction in passenger rates to the World's Fair because they said that, if they did, they would be unable to handle the traffic that would result. When the New York Central proposed to put on twenty-hour trains between New York and Chicago, it was opposed by the other trunk lines. As an official of the

* See ANNALS OF THE AMERICAN ACADEMY, vol. i., pp. 103, 462.
† See Acworth. *Contemporary Review, 1891.*

Pennsylvania road said, "such a train presents no difficulties to the Pennsylvania Railroad Company from a mechanical standpoint, nor from the standpoint of the road's condition. But as regards running such a train in its relation to our other business it would be prejudicial to those interests. The volume of freight and passenger business over the Pennsylvania is simply enormous, and the running of such a train would seriously interfere with its movement, especially at the present time, when the road from New York to Chicago is crowded with business."* The coal lines of the East are crowded to such an extent that passenger trains are often delayed, and shippers rendered unable to secure the prompt delivery of freight. Under present conditions the large increase of local and distance traffic which it is possible for cheapness to produce would involve greater outlays of capital than the increased traffic receipts would justify, but were the railroads relieved of a good share of their bulky freight, they might, with very small outlay of capital, greatly develop the passenger business.

The increase and extension of waterways aid the railroads through the increased travel which results from building up manufactures, developing trade, and promoting the growth of large cities. Take, for instance, the influence of that greatest of all inland waterways, the Great Lakes, on the growth of the passenger traffic in the States bordering the lakes. It has been, in large part, the improvement of the harbors and channels of the Great Lakes that has caused the phenomenal growth of Duluth, Milwaukee, Chicago, Detroit, Toledo, Cleveland, Buffalo, etc. The railroads have not only aided the growth of these cities, but have in turn been greatly benefited through the development which has come to them by means of the improvements of the water route. Indeed, the most important railroad systems of the United States are those which share in the commerce of the region round about the Great Lakes.

* *Public Ledger*, Philadelphia May 11, 1893.

This fact reveals the true relation of the two agents of commerce. They are complements of each other. When the waterway and railroad are perpendicular, they feed one another; when they run parallel, competition results in reciprocal development of each—at least, will so result when the waterway corresponds, as to dimensions and equipment, to the commercial needs of the present, and provides for the transportation of goods through comparatively long distances. The Rhine Valley, as well as our own lake region, furnishes an illustration of this truth. The statistics of the traffic during the last forty years on the Rhine River and on the railroads of the Rhine Valley, show that the growth of the transportation on each has been about equally rapid. "Neither of the two means of communication has prevented the development of the other." *

Though the railroads and waterways ought to be competitive means of transportation, they ought not to antagonize each other. Only the benefits which the railroad receives from the waterway have been cited; but the aid is reciprocal. The well-located and well-constructed waterway need not fear co-ordination with the railway, indeed, the attainment of the highest degree of usefulness is otherwise impossible. The railroad must be present to aid in distributing the finished products manufactured from the articles transported by water, or there will be but small freight by water. Not only these manufactured goods but such articles of consumption as pass directly from the waterway to the consumers must be distributed by the railway, for water routes are few in number and reach, directly, but a very limited number of consumers. The general relation of waterways and railroads, as collectors and distributers respectively, is shown by the shipments into and out of Paris by water and by rail in 1890. The waterways brought to Paris 4,037,719 tons, and the railroads 5,826,548 tons, the percentage carried by each being 41 per cent and

* Van der Borght, p. 25. "Report on Railways and Waterways" to Fifth International Congress on Inland Navigation.

59 per cent respectively; but of the freight from Paris, which, of course, consisted mostly of manufactured articles, the waterways carried only 953,834 tons, while the railroads transported 2,335,252 tons, the percentages being 29 per cent and 71 per cent respectively.* This took place, however, with very poor connections at the ports between the waterways and the railroads, so poor, indeed, as to greatly limit trans-shipment. The close connection of the waterway with the railroad, so that shipment from one to the other may be easily accomplished is hardly less essential to the waterway's best use than the improvement of the way itself. The people of Philadelphia have recognized this fact. A belt line railroad is being built by which the railroads entering the city may each reach the wharves throughout the length of the Delaware and Schuylkill water-fronts. The advantage of this will be great, alike to railroads and inland waterways centering at Philadelphia; vessels from the inland as well as from the ocean will be able to exchange freight with the railways.

This discussion of the complementary character of the two means of transportation, prepares the way for the consideration of the relation of inland waterways to State-owned railroads, of the influence of the former on the tariffs and revenues of the latter. All the advantages which have been cited above as accruing to private roads from the development of routes of inland navigation flow to State railroads, and in a higher degree, because of the possibility of a more perfect co-ordination of the two means of transportation. As in the case of private so with State railroads, the waterway can relieve them of the traffic which is as well or better adapted to carriage by water, and leave the road free to expand its fast freight business and passenger traffic without making the large investments of capital that would be otherwise necessary in order to widen the roadbed, increase the number of tracks, and enlarge terminal yards and stations. The existence of

* See Delaunay—Belleville, p. 27. Report to Fifth International Congress on Inland Navigation.

both means of transportation would thus make possible an economical division of traffic, that would give to each way the carriage of those things which it was best fitted to transport under the conditions existing at the time the freight was offered for shipment. This has to a large extent taken place in the Rhine Valley, and will do so more in the future, as the waterways are developed and their co-ordination with the railroads is made more complete.

The division of freight between the two means of transportation is not, of course, into two distinct classes—one class going by water and one by rail—for each agent carries many kinds of articles that the other does. Still the waterway reduces the ratio which the bulkier goods would otherwise bear to the more profitable classes of rail freight, and this is to the advantage of the net returns on the capital invested in railroads.

The State, furthermore, by extending inland waterways, would save not alone in amount of necessary investment in railroads, but also in expenses of operation relatively to gross receipts. As was seen, the costs of operation are a very large share of the gross receipts from the freight that would mostly go to the waterway, and the waterway would enable the railroad to develop a kind of traffic where net receipts above costs of operation are larger. Thus it comes about that both burdens of expense which the railroads must meet, interest on investment and cost of operating, are rendered lighter when the waterways co-operate with the railroads in the transportation of freight. The development of inland navigation has also been shown to increase rather than to lessen the volume of traffic by rail. Waterways, therefore, enable the State to reduce tariffs on its railroads and still receive as large a net return on their business as would be possible without the traffic by water.

Because of the fact that the inland waterways and the State railways of Prussia are under the control of different officials there has been a good deal of rivalry between the two means of communication. The managers of the railroads have been anxious to show a surplus, and have opposed the extension of inland waterways. Of late this opposition seems to have weakened. Prussia has entered upon the construction of canals, and the connection of the two means of transportation has been made closer, without detriment either to the traffic or net receipts of the railroads. The Prussian Minister of Public Works, Thielen, said, in 1891 : "The subsequent development of the railway service must go on simultaneously with the improvement of the navigable ways. The navigable way is the sister, equal by birth, of the railway."

The commercial position of the waterway, and its influence on the tariffs and revenues of the railroad are well stated by the following resolution of the Fourth International Congress on Inland Navigation: "The existence and development together of railways and waterways is desirable, first, because these two means of transport are the complements of each other and ought to contribute each according to its special merits to the public good ; second, because viewed broadly, the industrial and commercial development which will result from the improvement of the means of communcation must in the end profit both railways and waterways."

CHAPTER VII.

UNDER WHAT CONDITIONS AND TO WHAT EXTENT CANALS CAN COMPETE WITH RAILROADS IN THE FUTURE.

Mention was made in a previous connection of the necessity for singling out the canal from other inland waterways for the purposes of special study. In this chapter improved rivers and lakes are dropped from discussion, in order thereby to make a more critical analysis of the commercial position of the purely artificial waterway and of its relation to the railway. Herein lies the most difficult problem of inland navigation, the one concerning which there is the greatest dispute. It is, however, with no desire to enter the arena of disputation, but with the purpose of setting forth in an analytical way the most recent and salient facts about the canal that this chapter is written.

In entering upon this analysis it is necessary to bear in mind that there are at least three very distinct kinds of canals. There are those with capacity and equipment for floating the ships that ply the ocean and such large interior lakes as make up the chain along our northern boundary; then there are canals whose construction, breadth of way and locks make them navigable by the large steamers of shallow draft that run on the large rivers; finally, there is the barge canal, the waterway which the word canal first calls up in the minds of most persons. This third kind requires a depth equal to or greater than is necessary for river boats, but its other dimensions may be smaller. The traction of canal barges has been, and is even to-day, generally horse power; that, however, was not a necessary condition of barge canal traffic; in the future steam, or perhaps electricity, will in the case of the waterway as elsewhere be the prevailing motive power. It is obvious that these three kinds of canals fulfill different services to commerce and do not each stand in the same relation to other means of transportation.

Concerning the power of the canal large enough to float the ocean ships and deep-draught lake vessels to compete with the railroads when once it is completed there is no doubt, provided the waterway is in the line of an important and growing commerce. Whether or not realizable tolls will return good interest on invested capital depends, of course, on the circumstances of its construction and the traffic that it secures. On this ground alone capitalists decide whether they will put money into any enterprise. States or cities will not neglect this consideration, but will also act in large part on other motives, and in the case of such great works as the construction of these largest-sized canals the interests affected are so varied and the benefits so far-reaching that the general welfare of society makes it desirable that the State, either in its local or national organization, should insist that considerations other than the single one of profits on capital invested should decide whether or not a work should be executed.

Against the benefits which will result from the construction of a canal or a railroad must be measured the costs of putting the work in condition for use and the subsequent expenses of operation and maintenance. What the benefits of each way really are must be kept clearly in mind. The preceding pages have shown that the rail and water routes perform different kinds of service, not only as carriers, but as developers of traffic, and have emphasized the fact that the importance of the waterway and its relation to the railroad are not to be discovered by merely comparing the tonnage statistics of the two.

The cost of constructing a canal depends on the character of the country through which it is run and on the dimensions and equipment that it is given; while these last must be determined by the use to which the waterway is to be put. If the canal is to extend the commerce of the ocean or the largest lakes, it must be deep enough to allow ocean vessels and large lake ships to navigate it, and be large enough to handle the traffic to be moved. Such a waterway may sometimes cost a very large sum, and at the same time justify the expenditure. The Manchester Canal will cost about $2,000,000 a mile. This is, of course, several times what the best equipped four-tracked railroad would cost; but the waterway will not only be capable of performing as great a service as such a railroad, and at a far cheaper rate, but will do for the commerce of Manchester much that no railroad could perform. It will make Manchester a seaport. Likewise, in the case of a canal from the Great Lakes to the ocean, or from the Mississippi to the Great Lakes, it is quite useless to compare its costs with the expense of constructing a railroad. Such canals render a larger service, and a different one, than the railroad.

Whether the construction of a canal, be it large or small, is warranted or not, must be decided by considering the various benefits private and public that will flow from the investment of the capital necessary to execute the work. The costs can only be determined by careful estimates of the work actually required for the execution of the particular waterway. But little is to be gained by investigating the costs of existing canals, they are in most cases too small and too inadequately equipped. Future canals must be larger and be more substantially built, and will, therefore, cost much more than former ones.* Perhaps the only really helpful general principle that can be laid down is this: The larger canals are the more profitable investments they will be, provided they are used to their entire capacity. Of course, this principle is usually true of the railroad business, the exceptions arising in the case of those lines, so located, that they can increase the number of

---

* The Prussian consulting architect Michaelis, in 1882, submitted estimates of the costs required to construct four canals, having a total length of 354 miles, and capable of floating boats of 500 tons burden. The outlay per mile according to his estimate would be $84,162. This is surprisingly low; and cannot be taken as applicable to countries more hilly than Prussia.

their tracks only by exceptionally expensive works of construction, or can acquire larger terminal facilities only at great costs. These conditions could hardly obtain with a waterway. If it is possible to build a waterway at all of moderate depth and size, its construction with larger dimensions would nearly always be possible. Furthermore, the traffic-bearing capacity which would result to the waterway from giving the canal the larger size, would be proportionally greater per dollar of investment than the traffic-bearing capacity which would result from money spent in constructing the waterway with small proportions. The difference between the costs of a small canal and a large one lies chiefly in expenses of excavation; and of course, this is only one of the items of cost. The other items, locks, protection of banks, construction of wharves, etc., increase in cost at a diminishing rate as the canal is enlarged in its carrying capacity.* As will be shown later, traction and other expenses necessary to navigation decrease rapidly with the size and depth of the waterway.

As regards the relative costs of maintaining an important railroad and a waterway after they have been constructed, the canal has the advantage over the railroad. Those canals of the present time whose construction permits of only slow navigation by horse traction are maintained at much less expense per mile than the railroads. The simplicity of the construction of the canal, and the small amount of wear and tear caused by the slow moving traffic make the expenses connected with maintaining a waterway small. Steam or electric traction, and higher rate of navigating will necessitate a more solid construction of the waterways, and will doubtless add somewhat to the costs of maintenance. The true basis for comparing the relative costs of maintenance of railways and canals consists in contrasting the expenses for maintenance incident to the transportation of equal volumes

---

*See *inter alia* "Canals and Their Economic Relation to Transportation." Lewis M. Haupt. Papers of American Economic Ass'n. Vol. v., No. 3.

of traffic. Granting the two ways to be of equally good construction the waterway must suffer less injury than the railroad from the friction incident to equal volumes of traffic.

Likewise the costs of moving freight by water are less than by rail. Here there are two items to be compared, costs of traction, and expenses due to floating and rolling stock. The fundamental reason why traction by water is less than by rail is sufficiently obvious. A horse can draw at the rate of three feet a second a load of about 3200 pounds on a good wagon road; of 30,000 pounds on a rail track, and from 120,000 to 200,000 pounds on the water. Where boats having steam engines as efficient as the railroad locomotive, are used in moving freight, as is the case on the ocean and the Great Lakes, the great economy of hauling by water becomes manifest. Boats carrying 2700 tons are run from Duluth to Buffalo in three and a half days at an average per diem cost of $120. Taking the distance to be about 1000 miles the cost per ton mile is only .015 cents. Let this be compared with the expenses of "conducting transportation" (exclusive of maintenance of way, structures, and equipment), assignable to freight traffic on the Pennsylvania Railroad, which are about 17 cents, or ten times as large as on the lake steamers, and the economy of water transportation under favorable conditions becomes evident.

The relation of net to "dead" load on boats and trains is another reason for the cheaper transportation by water. The net load of a ship is usually three or four times the weight of the boat, the larger the vessel the greater the ratio. The net load of a car is from one and a half to twice the weight of the car. This difference is increased by the fact that cars are generally not so fully loaded as are boats. The wagons used in the general merchandise traffic of England are seldom loaded to a third of their capacity. The railroads find that promptness of delivery makes it impossible to fill the wagons. The water traffic, on the other hand is not fast freight and boats can be fully loaded. On the fourteen principal waterways of Germany in 1887, eighty per cent of the boat loads were full cargoes. *

In the matter of cost and maintenance of equipment for moving freight, also, the waterway has a decided advantage over the railroad. A ship costs about one-fifth as much as a train, or as trains of cars of equal carrying capacity, whereas, the life of the ship is longer and the expenses of maintenance less. The canal barge of 500 tons burden has as great capacity as a good-sized train, and three times that of the average train of the United States. The enormous trains of 1200 and 1500 tons load run on the trunk lines are quite exceptional.

The average costs of moving a ton of freight a mile on the railroads of the United States (exclusive of costs of maintenance of way and structures), was .522 cents in 1890; the cost on the Pennsylvania was .390 cents; on the New York Central and Hudson River, .460 cents; on the Erie, .368 cents; on the Reading, .391 cents. Over against these figures may be placed the average freight rate of .135 cents, charged per ton mile on the traffic carried on the Great Lakes, a free natural waterway. Of course, it is not to be forgotten, that the costs of transportation on the Great Lakes are lower than they are, or can be, in canals. The average grain rates, in 1891, from Buffalo to New York by way of the Erie Canal and Hudson River, were 3.49 cents a bushel, or about .233 cents per ton mile. The distance from Albany to New York is covered by the Hudson River, where, of course, the cost of transportation is cheaper than by canal; but the Erie Canal is far from being such a waterway as those of the future will be. Most towing is still by animals, and boats have a capacity of only 240 tons burden, and are raised and lowered by comparatively small locks. It is safe to say, that the cost of transporting heavy freight on a well-equipped American canal, with boats of 500 tons burden

* J. Stephen Jeans. Report to the Fourth International Congress on Inland Navigation.

propelled by steam, will be less rather than more than .233 cents per ton mile—the grain rates between Buffalo and New York.

While it is true that the costs of transportation on canals must be more than on large lakes and rivers, the difference will be less in the future than at present. Indeed, when the waterway is an integral part of a system of natural watercourses, and has dimensions large enough to allow the boats that ply the natural waterways to navigate it, and when its banks are so protected as to make possible the use of steam-motor power (and these are the conditions that future canals must meet), then costs of moving freight on them will not be much higher than on the natural waterways.

No American engineers have made detailed calculations for the purpose of comparing how much railroad companies and owners of private canals must charge per ton mile of freight in order to obtain a fair remuneration on invested capital. Work of this kind has been done by the German engineers, Bellingrath and Symphner. They figured out carefully the cost of transportation by barge canals and by rail, including every item, the interest on all capital invested, the expenses for maintenance and management of ways, and for maintenance of floating and rolling stock, cost of hauling and profits of ship owners, but their calculations were confined to German roads and canals, and were made ten years ago. They do not throw much light on the relations of canals and railroads in another country as different from Germany as America. Industrial conditions also have changed not a little during the past decade. The calculations were not without value in as much as they show that ten years ago in Germany, barge canals capable of floating boats of 350 to 500 tons burden could carry bulky freight in large quantities much cheaper than the railroads.*

* *Cf.* Bellingrath "*Studien über Bau und Betrieb eines deutschen Kanalnetzes.*" Symphner "*Transportkosten auf Eisenbahnen und Kanälen.*"
August Meitzen "*Die Kanalfrage in Preussen*" in Schmoller's *Jahrbuch für Gesetzgebung und Statistik.* 8 b. 1884.

It is to be borne in mind that in making these comparisons between the costs of rail and water transportation the two ways are necessarily considered as performing the same service. This is, of course, one way to view the relation of the two means of communication. This shows that there is a large amount of freight that can be shipped more cheaply by water. But from what was said in Chapters V. and VI. it is evident that this is but one side of the question. The relation of the waterway to the railroad and to transportation and trade is more complex than that would imply. The fact has, perhaps, been sufficiently enforced, but it can hardly be too strongly emphasized, that the waterway does more than effect a saving of a few mills a ton on a part of the bulky freight shipped. The waterway has far-reaching indirect effects on industry, it is the complement of the railroad, and neither means of transportation can reach its highest usefulness to commerce without the presence of the other.

The canal may be said to be at present in a state of transition to a condition of greater efficiency. Important improvements are being made whose effect can be little less than a revolution of the canal as a means of transportation. Doubtless the change that first suggests itself as necessary in the equipment of the canals is the substitution of steam for horses as the motor power for the traction of boats. "The competition between canal and railway in this country never, in any fair sense, resulted in a victory of land carriage over water carriage; the victory was that of the steam engine over horse flesh, and very poor horse flesh at that." * Up to the present time most inland canals have been constructed for a small barge traffic, and the prevailing power used for moving boats has been horses. The reason why steam has not been substituted is that the construction neither of the waterway nor of the barge permitted it to be done. The width and depth of the old canals are not great enough; the banks are entirely

* Roberts, p. 5. Report on "Respective Uses of the Waterways and Railways of the United States" to the Fifth International Congress on Inland Navigation.

unprotected, or only partially secured against the attacks of waves generated by boats; the locks are too small and too numerous; and the blunt-ended, piston-like form of the old style of boats is such as to admit only of the slow motion of horse towing without piling up a cushion of water ahead of the barge. The general use of steam as a locomotive power on canals cannot take place until radical changes have been made both in the waterway and in the boats used on them.

How to protect the banks of canals in the best and cheapest way against the action of the waves is receiving much attention from engineers. In the case of the maritime Nord-Ost-See Canal masonry work of different kinds, depending on the material that is most accessible, is being used at a cost of about $20,000 a current mile of the canal. The costs in this canal are large, because much of the stone and brick has to be brought from a distance. The protection of the banks of smaller canals is less expensive, and probably woodwork, either of the character now used in the Netherlands and France or in some other form, can be employed successfully and at a less expense. *

The economy of steam traction even on canals of small dimension is beyond question. Mr. Hannan, Superintendent of Public Works of New York State, says that whatever profit was derived from the carrying trade on the Erie Canal in 1891 was made by those who operated steam boats. The results of Symphner's calculations were that steam power is sixteen and two-thirds per cent cheaper than well-organized animal traction for barges of 350 and 500 tons' burden. The larger the dimensions of the canals and the capacity of the boats the greater will be the economy of steam traction.

The best form of traction on a barge canal such as the Erie is still an undecided question. Several kinds have been successfully tried on different European canals. The

* For a discussion of methods of consolidating canal banks consult the papers on the subject submitted by Schlichting, Peslin, Van der Sleyden, Hoerschelmann to the Fifth International Congress on Inland Navigation.

navigation of the canal presents very different conditions from those that obtain on rivers. There the kind of a steamer to be used depends on the depth of the river and the swiftness of the current. In the lower reaches of a river the screw steamer is best; in the middle courses, where the current is more rapid and the possible draft of the boat small, the paddle steamer is the most efficient; where the current of the river is very rapid the chain steamer can be used most successfully. The chain steamer propels itself by means of a chain lying on the bed of the stream. The chain passes over the boat and about a drum which is revolved by an engine on the boat. Such chains have been laid in many of the rivers of Europe, the Seine, the Rhine, the Neckar, the Elbe and the Oder and others.

The difficulties connected with a shallow draft of water and with overcoming currents do not exist in canal navigation; here the problem is chiefly how to prevent the boats from creating waves destructive of the canal. Screw and paddle steamers are out of the question on canals with unprotected banks, and even those which have protected ones suffer more or less from the waves of steamers. Of chain steamers there are two kinds, the one described above, and the one which propels itself by means of an endless chain which the boat carries along. As the endless chain is being passed over the boat by the engine on the boat a part of the chain rests on the bed of the waterway, the weight of the chain being sufficient to enable the steamer to drive itself forward. The chain steamer avoids the creation of waves other than those due to its own motion. It affords a simple and economical power, but the breaking of the chain and the delay caused by the passing of boats cause a good deal of hindrance, and render the chain steamer somewhat unsatisfactory. Furthermore the most economical use of the chain steamer, the same as other steamers depends on the possibility of increasing the speed above that attained by animal traction, and this necessitates canals of considerable size with protected banks. This last condition holds equally true as regards the hauling of boats from the banks by locomotives or by means of a moving cable. Both of these methods of hauling from the bank have been experimentally tried with fair success. Of course the object here also has been to apply steam power in such a way as to do least damage to the unprotected or poorly protected canal banks, and, this being the case, it is probable that, as canals are built with banks well secured against the action of the waves, this makeshift method will be abandoned for the screw steamer, the one most used in all waters but those of shallow rivers. The probability of this taking place is increased by the fact that in the future the distinction between barge canals and those connecting segregated lakes and rivers will doubtless grow less and canals become more and more integral parts of improved natural waterways. Lake and river ship canals must, of course, be constructed with a depth and breadth of way and a solidity of banks that will permit lake and river steamers to navigate them.

There is a possibility that barge traffic on canals will be able to make use of electricity as a motor with more economy than steam. There is no reason why the trolley system should not be applied to the hauling of canal boats, the same as street cars, provided, the boats can be run at frequent and regular intervals as the cars are. It has been suggested that a trolley line be run along the Erie Canal, where these necessary conditions exist. The scheme could probably be carried out and result in an economy in costs for haulage, and produce an increase of traffic. The discussion of electricity, however, as a motor for barge canals, and the influence it would have on commerce, would better be postponed till some experiments have been made.

Mention has been made several times in this monograph, of the necessity for constructing canals larger than those of the past have been. The economy in traction and costs of transportation, generally deserves further emphasis. In the first place, attention may be recalled to the fact that, the larger the boat the greater the net, as compared to the dead, load to be hauled. Second, the cost of hauling the boat, exclusive of cargo, increases much slower than the tonnage capacity. For instance, the charges for hauling boats on the Saale River, Germany, between the mouth of the stream and the City of Halle, are twelve cents a kilometre for boats of thirty tons, and only thirty-four cents—less than three times as much—for boats of 300 tons, ten times as large. Third, the total costs of transportation decrease rapidly with the increase in the size of the cargo. Professor Lewis M. Haupt lays down the law that, "the cost of movement on water is inversely proportional to the draft of the vessel."* He bases his law on the following facts: The cost of carrying goods on the Erie Canal in boats of less than five feet draft, is 3.00 † mills a ton mile; on the Great Lakes in boats drawing fourteen to sixteen feet, the costs are 1.2 mills; on the ocean in ship drawing twenty-five feet, .5 mills. The reciprocals of the drafts of the vessels—$\frac{1}{5}$, $\frac{1}{15}$, $\frac{1}{25}$—are to each other in the ratio 1, .33, .2; and the freight charges—3, 1.2, .5—are in the ratio 1, .4, .17—the two ratios being nearly the same.

The construction of larger canals entails the enlargement and improvement of locks. How to overcome differences in level has always been a difficult problem in canal construction and navigation. Before the invention of the chamber lock—probably about the beginning of the sixteenth century—artificial waterways were possible in only a few places. The lock continues to be the method of overcoming differences in level that is usually made use of, and though it has been much improved, as will be seen, it still offers a great drawback to commerce on the canal, one that men are willing to make great sacrifices to avoid. The lock, especially such

* "Canals and their Economic Relation to Transportation." p. 65. Papers of the American Economic Association, vol. v, No. 3. Many conclusions of this work (as is the case generally with Professor Haupt's writings) are based on insufficient data. The force of his arguments is often weakened by claiming to much for them.

† This does not deny the fact that there are boats running, which draw six feet of water and carry for less than three mills.

as has been constructed in the paston barge canals, imposes serious limitations on the efficiency of the canal. They raise and lower vessels only a few feet—eight feet, ten inches, in the case of the Erie Canal—thus they require numerous lockings to raise or lower a boat through large differences of level. This, of course, takes much time. The navigation routes of England, independent of the railroads, have on an average a lock to every mile and a half of their length; those canals owned by the railroads average a lock to every one and a fifth miles. More than a third of the time spent in navigating English canals is spent in passing the locks. The only way by which this is to be avoided is to reduce the number of locks and concentrate them at fewer points. This would both reduce the time spent in locking boats and increase the distances of unimpeded navigation. The locking of a boat, further, requires the use of a good deal of water, even though the waste has been much reduced by various devices, and makes the "feeding" of some inland canals a serious problem.

In order to avoid the hindrances which locks place upon the navigation of barge canals attempts have been made to substitute some better way of raising and lowering ships; and with the result that two new methods have been successfully employed in a few places to raise and lower barges. These two new methods are the perpendicular hydraulic lifts, and inclined planes.

By the hydraulic lift, boats are raised and lowered in caissons. Each lift has two caissons, each resting on one or more hydraulic rams. The two caissons rise and fall alternately, the motive power being supplied by having more water in the descending caisson than in the ascending one. The inclined plane is an arrangement whereby the canal boat is carried on a carriage up or down an inclined plane from one level to another. The hydraulic lift and inclined plane succeed in avoiding the objections which obtain against the lock. The differences in level overcome by them are several times as great as by the lock. The amount of water wasted when the lift or inclined plane is used is only a fraction as much as when the lock is employed; and the ascents or descents from one level to another may be concentrated at a few points in the canal, instead of being scattered throughout its entire course.

Both the hydraulic lift and the inclined plane have been successfully constructed and operated. The inclined plane on the Shropshire Canal, of England, effects a perpendicular rise of 213 feet; there are, also, inclined planes on the Bute Canal, of England. The first perpendicular lift constructed for raising and lowering canal boats was the one at Anderton, England, by which boats of 100 tons cargo are taken from the Trent and Mersey Canal and raised fifty feet into the Weaver River. There is a lift at Fontinètte, France, which raises and lowers vessels of 350 tons forty-four feet. On the Belgian Canal du Centre, near Louvière, there are, within a distance of seven kilometres, four lifts which together overcome a fall of 222 feet. In Germany, five small inclined planes have been constructed on the canals; but no lifts have as yet been built. "It is probable, however, that hydraulic lifts will be included in the plans for the canals that have been projected from Lübeck to Lauenburg, and from Dortmund through Minden to Magdeburg."* There is one canal in the United States, the Morris and Essex in New Jersey, on which an inclined plane is in use. No lifts have been constructed on any canals of the United States; but the construction of two is contemplated to aid in overcoming the obstructions to navigation at the Dalles in the Columbia River, Oregon.

Of the two arrangements for raising and lowering canal barges, the hydraulic lift and the inclined plane, the latter has more merits; for there is practically no limit to the difference in level it can overcome. Again, the inclined plane costs less, and is not so complex a structure. Neither the

* Quoted from a letter written by Bellingrath, February 10, 1892.

lift nor the plane however will displace the use of the lock to any great extent even for raising and lowering barges. The large sized barges that will come into use on the larger canals of the future, would require a lift of very expensive construction to raise and lower them. The lift will probably never be used to any great extent to raise and lower ocean and lake steamers. The inclined plane will probably be used where barges and river boats are to be carried through great differences of level, and in other places where canals have a small supply of water. Except in these very unusual cases the lock will be used; indeed, given a sufficient supply of water, the locks as now improved are able to raise and lower vessels through long distances. Some of the locks on the Nicaragua Canal are to have a lift of 45 feet. They are all 80 feet wide and 650 feet long. The locks as designed by Col. Blackman for the canal were to be 700 feet long, 100 feet wide, and effect lifts from 50 to 100 feet.*

The usefulness of the canal, and the importance of its service as compared with those rendered by the railroad, depend to no small degree on the way in which it is administered. The waterway should be kept open to navigation as much as possible, and all closings on account of the climate, or for making repairs should be reduced to a minimum. In regions where the frost closes navigation for a part of the year, repairs should be made during the winter. In many instances the improvement in harbor facilities, the enlargement of wharfage space, and the use of machinery for loading and unloading boats, will render an important aid to inland navigation. A boat on the Elbe spends seventy-five of the three hundred days of the season of navigation in motion, and the other two hundred and twenty-five days in the docks. As a contrast to this may be mentioned the steamship "Monola" on the Great Lakes, which spent, in 1891, 175 days sailing and only 47 lying in port. Most of all ought the harbors to provide better facilities for reshipment from railroad to

* See Jeans "Waterways and Water Transportation." pp. 419-420.

waterway and *vice versa*. The best possible co-ordination ought to exist between the two means of transportation ; it is only thus that they can fulfill their functions as complements of each other.

So far in this discussion of the relation of the canal to the railroad and of the improvements now being made in the waterway, and which will increase its commercial importance and its power to develop side by side with the railroad, the canal has been regarded merely as an agent of commerce ; but it often performs other services by draining or irrigating the country through which it passes. Much of Schleswick and Holland have been converted by canals from swamps into fertile fields. The canals and river improvements of Spain have aided in irrigation. As the regulation and improvement of the Po, Rhine and other rivers have had in mind the prevention of floods, so may the canals keep in view the agricultural interests of the country through which they run.

On the basis of the considerations elaborated in this and the preceding chapters, I feel convinced that the canal is capable of rendering industry and commerce important services. The maritime and lake-ship canals rank first in the value of their aid ; those extending or connecting large rivers, and so constructed as to form an integral part of the navigation on those streams come second in importance. As has been stated above, the barge canal, as distinct from the two other classes, will be constructed less frequently in the future than it has been in the past ; but the usefulness of such waterways under conditions modified to suit the needs of the present is not a thing of the past.

While this chapter was being written, the author received a letter from Ewald Bellingrath, of Dresden, to whom reference has been made in the foregoing pages. The opinions of "the best informed man on German inland commerce "* are : "The power of the canal to compete with the railroad

* Quoted from Symphner.

in regions where the difficulties are not too great is beyond doubt if, (1) a sufficient quantity of freight exists, or can be secured, for transportation ; (2) the canal be constructed with not too small proportions, ships not under 500 tons; (3) there be a good service to supply steam traction.''

Such are the conditions which must exist before a barge canal can become a valuable means of transportation. A large amount of freight, to be shipped a comparatively long distance ; dimensions of waterway and locks large enough, at least, to permit barges to carry 500 tons, a load about three times the average trainload in the United States, and about half the load of the heaviest trains ; such a construction of the banks of the canal as to make possible the use of steam traction. With these conditions fulfilled, the usefulness of the barge canal is assured. To whom its construction, and the construction of the other two kinds of canals should fall, depends on circumstances which will be considered in the next chapter.

CHAPTER VIII.

THE CONSTRUCTION OF CANALS AND THE IMPROVEMENT OF NATURAL INLAND WATERWAYS BY THE STATE AND BY CORPORATIONS.

In the foregoing chapters, the character and extent of the services now being rendered by the inland waterways have been indicated, and the present imperfections of the canal, and the possibility and probability of their being overcome in the near future, have been discussed. It has been further shown that under certain conditions the canal cannot only compete with the railway, but can perform some services much better. The present chapter has to do with the question who shall improve natural waterways and construct canals. Shall the State pay for and carry out these improvements; or shall it leave them wholly or in part to private enterprise?

In Germany the State carries on the work; the use of rivers is free, that of canals on payment of low tolls. The extension and improvement of inland waterways in France have in the past been at times individual and sometimes State enterprises; the State has, however, bought up most all private waterways, and since 1880, has maintained them at public expense for the free use of all. The waterways of Italy are, with one exception, State property, and not subject to tolls. The inland navigation of Belgium has been improved and extended by the State, and tolls are now collected. Russian waterways are improved and maintained entirely at the cost of the State. Works in England have been executed by corporations, or "trusts," sometimes with State aid, oftener with municipal help, and frequently with neither. The act of Parliament of 1888 extends the State's control of tariffs and tolls. The inland navigable ways of the United States have been extended by individuals and corporations,

CONSTRUCTION AND IMPROVEMENT OF WATERWAYS.

by the States, and by the Federal Government. Natural waterways and canals under the control of the United States are free. The same is true of the canals owned by New York; but on other canals tolls are levied. The discussion of the relation of the State to waterways involves two considerations: Who shall execute the work of improving waterways, and how shall these improvements be paid for? The questions will be answered in turn, in this and the following chapter.

In but few questions do all the advantages rest with one side. In the case of waterway improvements there are some arguments in favor of private enterprise. They are the following: (1) The State avoids a heavy expenditure of money; her taxes may be lighter, and the demands of her budget may be more easily met. (2) The State is spared an important increase in her civil service force, and this is a consideration not to be disregarded, especially by the United States. The functions of our Federal Government are increasing and must necessarily continue to do so rapidly with the development of our administrative powers, and we cannot help regarding with concern any increase in our civil list, until we see civil service reform drawing on apace. (3) The State should leave to the individual whatever he can do equally well. If there are improvements of waterways which individuals or corporations can make equally as well as the State, and with as much benefit to the public, the State should not undertake the work. The extensive assumption by the German States of industrial functions which other countries leave to individuals, has had a marked effect in checking and weakening the capability of individual initiative. German capitalists have not the daring and invention in undertaking and developing large business enterprises that those of England and America have. The Germans have grown to feel in a large degree dependent on State initiative in industry, a fact which explains in part why Germany is the land where socialism most flourishes. (4) Closely related to this is a fourth argument in favor of individual enterprise. The management of private business is less bureaucratic, and where competition exists, tends to adapt itself more to commercial wants. Competitive enterprises bid for trade, and seek to meet its wishes, while a bureaucracy is less flexible and compels business to adapt itself to administrative regulations. Too much, however, must not be made of this fact. A strong private monopoly may be quite as unyielding and regardless of public needs as a bureaucracy. (5) In leaving these works to private companies, the State avoids all danger of taxing one section of the country to favor another. The United States is a large country, and business interests are many and diversified. Not all sections of the country have exactly similar interests. The fact, however, is constantly becoming less important. With the increase in population, the development of industry, the growth in commerce due to the improvement and extension of means of communication, the development of banking and systems of credit, the solidarity of our social and industrial life grows ever stronger. The circles of influence exerted by an improvement in navigation extend wider with the increase in the solidarity of business interests.

(6) It is often urged in favor of private enterprise that it is much more certain than the State to commence only those works which promise a return on capital invested—that there will be greater economy in investment and expenditure. This argument, however, cannot bear up against criticism. If the proneness of men to speculate be considered and the very small percentage of all business men which the successful ones comprise, be taken into consideration, it becomes impossible to maintain that the improvement of waterways by individuals instead of by the State will be any safeguard against waste of capital. Indeed, experience in this matter is favorable to State enterprise. The private capital was injudiciously invested quite as freely as public funds during "the canal mania" on works that have since become of little use or have been abandoned. It was not

the French government which wasted its money on the Panama project.

The reasons in favor of State, as compared with private, improvement and extension of waterways are: (1) The fact that water routes are from their nature public ways, and whether the works on them be executed by the State or by corporations, the State ought to maintain the public character of the waterway. This demands State supervision to the extent of fixing dimensions of canals and river channels, of controlling tolls and tariffs, and of laying down rules in accordance with which the waterways shall be administered. The State can much more easily and surely maintain the water routes as public highways by improving and extending them herself. The experience of England, where nearly all these works have been private enterprises, has, as has already been shown in another connection, been anything but satisfactory. The English canals have already been discussed, but their condition may, at this point, be referred to again with profit. It will be best to quote the words of an Englishman:* "Take as a case in point the transport of iron between London and Liverpool, or *vice versa*. In this freight the trader would have to deal with no fewer than six canal administrations to Preston Brook, within twenty miles of Liverpool, where it would have to be transhipped and carried for the remainder of the distance on the Bridgewater Canal. Until recently, when the Bridgewater Canal became the property of the Manchester Ship Canal Company, they charged 7s. 6d. per ton for this service, or more than 2s. 4d. per ton more than the other six companies charged for a distance of 220¼ miles. The canal charges—between the two greatest ports in the world—was rather over a penny per ton per mile. This is only an example of the general character of the system as now organized, and it is not to be wondered at if, under such circumstances, traders are

* Jeans. Article in Report of the Fourth International Congress on Inland Navigation.

disposed to give canals a very wide berth. Singular as it may appear, an ocean steamer often conveys cargo across the Atlantic, a distance over 3000 miles, for a rate less by one-half than the charges by water transport by canal between London and Liverpool, a distance of only 240 miles, or about one-thirteenth of the distance."

(2) The services, other than those of navigation, which are rendered by improved waterways, will be better secured in the case of State enterprise. The improvement of the Po River system of Italy has had for its object the prevention of the inundations in the central and lower parts of the valley; and the State, by studying the character of the streams of the Lombard provinces, has improved them in such a way as to prevent, to a great extent, inundations in the provinces of Venice and Farara. The improvements of the Rhine, the Mississippi and other great rivers should aim more than they do at present to control the oft-recurring floods.

(3) Again, the improvement and extension of the most important inland waterways will progress more slowly than they ought, if left to individual enterprise, and commerce will thereby greatly suffer. It is doubtful whether private companies would have undertaken the improvement of the Mississippi River or the Great Lakes; and certainly they would not have begun the work so soon nor have executed it so thoroughly as has the United States government. Indeed, such works are not adapted to individual enterprise. Not so much because of the large amount of capital required, for to-day capitalists are not awed by the magnitude of any undertaking; but more because of the complicated legal relations that would arise were a private company to assume the work of improving such a navigable highway as the Great Lakes, for instance, over which several States and two nations exercise dominion. The improvement of the Mississippi system would involve equal difficulties. The fact, however, that militates most against private enterprise in

these particular instances is that both of the great systems of waterways ought to be improved together according to a common plan. This is something that the United States has not yet done, but ought to do. The improvement of the Mississippi River system and the Great Lakes ought to be under one and the same commission.

But were the character of the work to be executed such that it could be successfully carried out by private corporations, no country would think of giving over the improvement of the Mississippi River to a private company. To do this would place the commerce of a great natural waterway, in fact of a great river system, draining the vast region between the Allegheny and the Rocky Mountain ranges, under the influence, if not control of a few individuals. The same considerations would hold concerning the Great Lakes. Such a case is of course intrinsically very different from the improvement of a short English river on which only a few cities are located. Some canals also are much more clearly the work of the government than are others. One would hardly think of giving over the control of a lake-ship canal from the great lakes to the ocean to a private company, a canal which would be the key to the commerce of the entire northern part of the United States. The objection to the construction of a canal from St. Paul to Lake Superior by a private corporation or municipality is much less; such a canal would by no means be of merely local importance; but it is much more so than the one from the Great Lakes to the ocean would be. If it be granted that the Manchester Ship Canal may rightly be left by the English government to the City of Manchester and the Manchester Ship Canal Company, they being subject to careful legal restrictions, that is by no means evidence that a trans-national canal leading from London to Liverpool through Northampton, Birmingham, Newcastle, and other large cities, should be controlled by a private company, not to say several companies, as is at present unfortunately the case.

(4) The very forces that tend to cause the improvement of waterways to be executed by private persons, may furnish reasons why such works ought to be executed by the State. In England where the individual feels quite independent of the State, and views with suspicion any State interference with industry, the improvement of inland navigation has naturally been the work of corporations. In Germany, on the other hand, the relation of the State to industry is different. Individuals look to the State for the execution of these works. The thought finds characteristic expression in this sentence taken from report of the Prussian ministry in 1882: "In view of past experience, there is hardly any doubt that the State, in case any new project is to be carried out, must assume the construction at public expense."

Whether the State or corporations will most naturally undertake the improvement of inland navigation depends, as Professor Lujo Brentano, of Munich, says, "Upon a country's past political development and the power of individual initiative which that development has called forth. Where initiative power is strong, waterways will be constructed without the State; but where centuries of State intervention have killed all private initiative, foreign capitalists, if any, are the ones that do the work. The gas works and water works of Germany may be cited as an example of this." The policy that ought to be adopted in regard to the improvement of waterways depends, according to Professor Brentano, "upon present political conditions. Where the State is everything, the construction of waterways by private persons is better, otherwise, the party which has the control of the State in its hands, may manage the inland navigation in an absolute way. Where individuals are everything construction by the State is better, in order thereby to break the monopoly of private persons." *

* These two statements are a free translation of the following note made by Professor Brentano during a conversation the author had with him:

" Die Frage ob Staat oder Aktil ist nicht blos eine Frage gegenwärtiger Ökonomischer Zweckmässigkeit. Sie hängt ab: (1) Von vergangener politischer Ent-

The half of this argument which advocates State works in countries where private monoplies have overwhelming power is strong ; the other half seems less so. The sacrifice that Germany would make, were she to leave to private parties the improvement of her inland navigation would not be recompensed by the benefits she might thereby receive from the added initiative power of individual and from the curb placed upon the irresponsibility of a bureaucratic administration.

(5) Private ownership of other means of communication affords an added reason for State ownership of important waterways. The large influence of American waterways on railroad rates and the meagre power of English inland navigation in that direction have been considered. Competition between railroads can no longer be relied on as a controller of rates. Waterways must regulate them. If the navigable routes be operated by the State they can do so; if by corporations, as in England, they will combine with the railroads. Supplementary to this argument it may be added that the State ownership of railways is no reason against State waterways. Curiously enough a competition exists between the State railways and State waterways of Germany that has tended to force down rates. This, however, may be regarded as an accidental, rather than a necessary, relation. The chief advantage of the State ownership of both means of communication results from their co-ordination in such a way that each performs the commercial service it is best fitted for, and in such a way that each increases the usefulness of the other.

Whether the question be viewed from the standpoint of

wickelung und dem Mass der Initiative der Einzelnen, welche jene hervorgerufen hat. Wo Initiative, werden Kanäle auch ohne Staat gebaut. Wo Jahrhunderte von Staatseinwirkung alle private Initiative ertödtet haben, sind es höchstens fremde Kapitalisten, die bauen. Vgl. die Gas- und Wasseranstalten in Deutschland. (2) Von gegenwärtigen politischen Verhältnissen. Wo Staat alles ist, ist Kanalbau durch Private besser, sonst tyrannisirt die Partei, die den Staat in Händen hat, auch die Kanalschifffahrt. Wo Private alles sind, Bau durch Staat, um Monopol der Privaten zu brechen."

I have translated "Kanal" by waterway, because that expresses the thought Professor Brentano had in mind.

theoretical advantages and disadvantages of State improvement and extension of inland waterways, or whether these theoretical considerations be modified by taking into account peculiarities in national temperament, and differences of present circumstances in various countries, the reasons for State construction of many works seem conclusive. The improvement of lakes and large rivers, and the construction of canals of large commercial importance, are clearly the duty of the State. The objection given above, that the functions of the State will thus be unduly augmented, has, on analysis, but little force. Where railways are in private ownership, it is the duty of the State to preserve the waterways as competitive routes of commerce; and when waterway improvements are made by private companies, the State can only do this, as the English experience clearly shows, by fixing the dimensions of artificial water-courses, by establishing rules for administering the waterway, and by controlling rates and tolls. The functions exercised by the State in this control of a waterway, must necessarily be many, and ownership adds to these offices little more than the increased taxation necessary to meet the expenses of construction. Whether it is possible for the State to control rates on private waterways in such a way as to maintain the competition with railroads that is desirable, may be doubted. England has failed, or nearly so, in this respect.

In the improvement of important lakes and large rivers, and in the construction of canals of wide commercial importance, the State cannot be charged with sectionalism. Still, as in the case of the United States, where nearly all improvements of waterways are made by the State, there is always the danger that the public will be taxed for the benefit of small sections. The United States and the several States have not always been careful enough in choosing works of a national character, and money has wrongly been spent on works of only a local importance. These local works have not only favored sections, but have involved a waste of capital. The United States and the several States in legislating regarding internal improvements, must ever be on their guard against works not of State or national importance. Local works should be left to localities or individuals.

The economical expenditure of money by the State demands both a thorough acquaintance on the part of the Legislature with the industrial conditions and needs of the country, and a knowledge of the ability of improved waterways to meet those conditions and needs. The character of the waterway that will best meet the requirements in a particular case, must also be known. An insufficient knowledge of the needs of trade, and of the means of transportation best calculated to meet those needs, has resulted in many unwise river improvements and canal constructions. To prove this, it is only necessary to point to the less important canals of France, which fall far short of paying interest on invested capital. The canals of Ohio and Indiana and other American States, were, in many cases, located and constructed without sufficient data. Many canals have been constructed, and even since the introduction of the railroad, where a cheap local railway would better have been placed, and would have been placed had the characteristics of the two agents of commerce been better known.

The real functions of inland waterways in commerce are now being studied, and are being better understood. Nothing else is doing so much to aid this study as the International Biennial Congresses on Inland Navigation. The fourth one of these congresses was held in Manchester, England, in 1890, and the fifth in Paris, August, 1892. The reports of their proceedings, and the papers presented are printed, both in English and French, and contain a rich mine of historical, statistical, and technical information regarding the inland navigation of the several countries of the world. It will have been noticed that the reports of the fourth and fifth congresses, have been made frequent use of in the preparation of this work. Reference has been made to the work done by the Commission on International Statistics of Inland Waterways, that was appointed by the Frankfurt Congress in 1888. The Fifth Congress which met in Paris, August, 1892, devoted a good deal of time to the consideration of the relation of waterways and railroads, and did much to emphasize the fact of their being complementary in character. The Sixth Congress will meet next year in Amsterdam. These gatherings bring together engineers prominent in official and in private life, and the discussions do much to promote a more scientific conception of the waterway as a means of transportation.

Waterways conventions, called to consider the needs of particular water routes and the benefits which their improvement will bring about, are a valuable agency in bringing to the attention of the public and of Congress the works whose promotion will do most to advance inland navigation. The more carefully and the more widely the relation of the important waterways to commerce is studied, the wiser will corporations and the government proceed with the works of improvement. A striking illustration of this is afforded by the convention which was held in Detroit, Michigan, December 17 and 18, 1891, to consider the question of a twenty and twenty-one foot waterway through the channels connecting the Great Lakes. The convention was suggested by Congressman Chipman. It was attended by delegates from six States and from Canada, representing boards of trade, shippers' associations, vessel owners, engineers in charge of the improvement of the lakes, and congressmen from the States contiguous to the lakes. The needs of the various parts of the Great Lakes were discussed, the relation of deep channels to the development of the lake commerce and to the industrial progress of the Northern States was considered, and the bearing of the lake transportation on the rate question was the subject of much consideration. The proceedings and papers of the convention, were printed and distributed in pamphlet form. The memorial to Congress had the effect of securing the appropriation necessary to carry out the work recommended by the convention.

A convention was called the year before at Evansville, Ind., to discuss the needs of the Mississippi River system, and the advantages that would follow its further improvement, and its connection with the Great Lakes. The importance of the subject is such that the convention ought to have had more influence than it had. The influence of the gathering would have been greater had it taken a wider view of the commercial interests involved and have gone less into details in the recommendation of numerous works of minor importance.

The apathy of New York State as regards the improvement of her canals led to the formation of "The Union for the Improvement of the Canals of the State of New York," with local unions throughout different parts of the State. The Central Union called a convention of delegates from the local unions to meet the nineteenth of October, 1892, to celebrate the centennial of the New York canals and to consider the further improvement of the State waterways and the importance of the work to the commercial interests of the State. Fifty-three organizations were represented by 596 delegates. The object of the convention was agitation, it is too early yet to look for definite results.

January 12, 1893, a convention met in Washington at the call of the Duluth Chamber of Commerce for the purpose of considering a deep-water ship canal from the Great Lakes to the sea. One hundred and twenty-five delegates were present. Chairman George H. Ely, of Cleveland, stated his platform to be "a waterway from the lakes to the sea over territory of the United States, independence of Canada, and cessation of legislation in favor of Canadian lines of transportation." He recommended that the convention do nothing more than to recommend Congress to make an appropriation for the survey of a route. The appropriation was not secured, however, at the last session of Congress.

Various conventions have been called in the interests of the Nicaragua Canal. The most important of these was the one that met at New Orleans, the thirtieth of November, 1892, at which delegates from every State and Territory in the Union were present. The purpose of the convention was to urge Congress to give its aid to the canal in order to secure the early completion of the work. The present condition of the canal and the reasons why the United States should lend the work its support will be considered in Chapter XII.

The value of such conventions as these is great. Wise legislation must proceed from the intelligence of the public. It may be thought by some that the influence of these gatherings will be to spur Congress on to excessive appropriations; it will rather be to temper action with knowledge and lessen the danger of misappropriations in the interest of sectionalism.

The position here taken in favor of the construction by the State of all great works of internal improvement, does not exclude private enterprise from works of local importance. On the other hand, the execution of local works should be left, as was stated above, to individuals or municipalities, the State, however, not neglecting, in any case, to maintain the public character of all waterways.

CHAPTER IX.

TOLLS ON WATERWAYS.

Vitally connected with the question whether or not corporations ought to improve inland waterways is the subject of tolls. Private waterways must needs charge tolls for their use by the general public. The conclusion of the preceding chapter was in favor of the construction of important waterways by the State, but the question still remains—How shall costs of improving, extending and maintaining inland waterways be paid? Should the public treasury bear the expense or should tolls be paid sufficient to cover the outlay? The subject brings the discussion into the realm of finance and involves some interesting points in theory.

Tolls are no longer collected on large rivers, and there is a movement to abolish them on canals. France and Italy have done away with all tolls. In Belgium "navigation dues are continually being reduced and their complete suppression seems rather a question of time and budget than of principle."* The rivers of Holland are free and the reduction of canal dues is probable. The abolition of tolls on the English canals is impossible so long as they remain private property; but the State regulates the dues. Most canals owned by the United States government are those constructed in connection with the improvement of natural waterways, but all are maintained for free use. New York abolished tolls on the canals when she purchased them. Ohio owns the canals within her boundaries, but charges tolls for their use. The same is true of Illinois as regards the Illinois and Michigan Canal. Most canals within the

---

* Dufourny, p. 16 of Article in Report of Fourth International Congress on Inland Navigation.

United States are private property and, of course, are not free waterways.

The movement for the abolition of tolls is prompted by a desire to promote inland commerce, and where such charges have been done away with, navigation has increased. The facts in regard to France were given in Chapter IV. The abolition of tolls on Italian waterways, also, "has increased the facility and amount of intercommunication."* Such a result is, of course, to be expected; but the question may be raised whether the abolition of tolls is in all cases necessary to a promotion of inland navigation, and whether this is the only way of accomplishing the desired end. If tolls may still rightly be charged on some waterways, what ones ought to be free and what ones not? According to what principle ought charges to be assessed?

Four principles may be made the basis of the charges which the government may require those to pay who use a public waterway: (1) The State may impose the charges with the intent of taxing inland navigation for the purpose of raising money, not only to maintain and improve her waterways, but also to help meet the general expenses of the State. In this case the maximum limit of the charges would be fixed at the point of the greatest productivity of the tax. (2) The State may regard the money invested in the improvement of inland navigation as a business enterprise on which a certain rate of profit ought to be obtained. If this view be taken, the charges will be fixed so as to secure this profit. In both these cases the State is taxing inland navigation, but the principles differ from each other in that different considerations determine the point of maximum charges. (3) The State may assess tolls on the principle of requiring navigation to pay the State for the labor that the State performs in making and maintaining improvements. In this case the State will fix the tolls so that it will be able just to recoup itself for actual expenses of construction and

* Bompiani, p. 3. *Ibid.*

maintenance. The State requires her waterways to be self-supporting—no more, no less. (4) The fourth principle, and the one on which several States now act, is to make no charges, but to improve, extend and maintain waterways at the expense of the general public.

Inland commerce is a very undesirable object of taxation. The State can hardly place taxes where they will be more burdensome. No State would to-day think of taxing inland navigation to the limit of maximum productivity of tax income, nor of imposing any heavy burden upon the commerce on her waterways. The wisdom of the State's trying to secure any profits on capital invested in the improvement of inland commerce for the purpose of replenishing the budget may be questioned. The Prussian government has, with doubtful propriety, turned a part of the surplus earnings of the State railroads into the general budget. The deficit in the finances might better have been covered by taxation, and the profits derived from the railroads have been used in developing the transportation system of the State. The primary object of the State in improving waterways, and building railroads, is to promote commerce and travel; tolls and tariffs high enough to yield profits will most surely do much to defeat that object; especially will this be so if the profits so obtained are not used in developing the means of communication and transportation. The State, then, ought to choose between the third and fourth principles, and either make inland navigation free or make such charges as will, in whole or in part, cover the outlay for construction and maintenance.

The State having decided that the waterways shall not directly contribute to the payment of other expenses than those the waterways themselves incur, the question of charges or no charges may be decided according to the general rule that *the incidence of the burden of expense should fall on those persons benefited, and, as nearly as possible, proportionally to the benefits received.* There are three classes which derive profit from the waterway. The general public, including producer and consumer, those who directly use the waterway, as shippers or carriers of freight on the waterway, and persons owning property along or near the line of the canal or improved river.

How shall these three classes be made to bear burdens proportionally to benefits? The improvement of great water courses like the Mississippi River and its important branches, the connection of two long water routes, the removal of the obstructions to commerce on a chain of great lakes, such as those in the north of the United States, and the extension of the commerce of these lakes to the Atlantic Ocean, all these are expenses which ought not to be borne, at least not more than partially borne, by the particular persons who make use of the waterway. The country, as a whole, receives most of the benefits of such improvements and it should pay most of their costs. Tolls on the commerce of such national waterways sufficient to cover all the expenses of improvement and maintenance would place the tax on only a part of the recipients of benefits and would at the same time place an undesirable restriction on commerce. The expenses ought, therefore, to be borne mostly by the United States and partly by the individuals who are the direct recipients of benefits.

The case of a canal leading from coal or iron mines in one part of a particular State to a large city in another part of the same State is different. Here the benefits to the United States, as a whole, are but slight, those of the particular State are greater, while the advantages gained by those who use the canal and by those who own property alongside or near it may be as great as in the case of a waterway of distinctively national importance; such a canal being of special value to the State, as a whole, within which it lies should be constructed and largely paid for by the State, rather than by the United States, or by those that make use of the canal after completion. The United States, however, would be justified in sharing a small part of the cost of constructing such a waterway, not only because the country at large receives certain benefits, but because the benefits, local and national, will be increased by such aid because of an earlier completion and better execution of the work.

In the case of canals, both of State and of national importance, individuals directly benefited ought to contribute toward meeting the expense. This could be accomplished in the case both of national and State waterways by taxing the increment in the value of the property along or near the canal due to the construction of the waterway. The justice of appropriating a part of this increment seems clear. Professor Meitzen, of the University of Berlin, says, "It may well be doubted whether it is right in principle to make the profits of a canal from the commerce on it bear alone the entire cost of construction."* The Prussian ministry expressed the same opinion in 1882.

Although this special taxation of individuals receiving the greatest benefits seems just, the method by which it may best be done is not so clear. The principle has long been carried out by cities in laying out and improving streets, and its application to waterway improvements is by no means impossible. One way of laying a burden on those receiving direct benefit from the canal by the increase in the value of property would be for the State to appraise the value of the property taken for the waterway and also the benefits conferred by the waterway on the owners of property alongside or near it. On the basis of such appraisal the contributions from those receiving direct advantage could be fixed by the State.

Though France has since 1880 maintained her waterways at public expense she has done something to distribute the expenses according to benefits. From 1880 to 1888 the costs were paid from an extraordinary budget whose funds were

* "*Die Kanalfrage in Preussen.*"

obtained by loans and from the surplus of the ordinary budget.* The Republic has been aided in some cases by the Departments. Most of the subventions by the Departments were paid by levying special taxes on interested parties. It has been proposed in France to establish Navigation Chambers which shall have control of the amelioration and utilization of navigable routes and have the power to levy special taxes to cover a part of the expenditures. Should this proposal be carried out it would retain the maintenance of navigable ways in the hands of the State, and at the same time secure a fuller sharing of expenses on the part of interested parties.

How the increment of property resulting from the construction of waterways may be taxed is a problem each State must solve for itself. The relation of the State to its several parts and to its citizens varies with each nation, and the commercial conditions are not the same in any two countries. The principle involved in taxing the increment is sound, the application of this principle should be the aim of legislation in the future more than it has been in the past.

The cost of constructing a local canal or improving a small water-course, in order, thereby, to connect two cities not distant from each other, or to bring a city in direct connection with a near-lying lake or ocean, may properly be left by the State to the individuals and cities directly interested, they being subject, as has been pointed out, to general legislation on the part of the State. On these waterways tolls or some other form of charges will, of a necessity, be laid.

To what extent the State, in the case of canal construction, should reimburse itself by means of tolls or other charges for first costs and for expense of maintenance has been partly answered. Great national water routes, both in the natural and artificial parts, should be free. The canals within a single State of the United States should be maintained—

---

* In theory, at least. In practice, however, a surplus of the ordinary budget would be hard to find.

not necessarily constructed—at the expense of the State as a whole, provided the benefits accrue to the State as a whole. To the extent that the benefits are merely private or local should the burdens of expense be shifted from the State, in order that the incidence of taxation may fall according to the rule previously laid down, that the burden of expense should fall on those that profit from the waterway, and, as nearly as possible, proportionally to the benefits received.*

The costs of constructing and maintaining inland waterways should, then, be met as follows: In all cases the property owners who receive direct benefits from the waterways should contribute toward the expense of construction; there should be no tolls on waterways of national importance, nor on those whose advantages accrue to all parts of a State; those which are primarily of value to particular parts of a State, and secondarily to other portions should be subject to moderate tolls sufficient to equalize burdens between the adjacent and distant localities according to benefits received.

The abolition of tolls on waterways is not necessary to their maintaining themselves as useful commercial agents. Waterways that have been wisely constructed and located are able to compete successfully with the railroad and perform important commercial services without the abolition of tolls. The considerations that should govern the assessment of charges on State waterways should be the healthy development of inland navigation and the equitable distribution of the expenses incurred.

* In the case of railway construction a division of burdens between the general and local governments has taken place in Prussia. As a condition of the construction of certain local roads and feeders the State requires those parties most interested to donate the land required for the road, and has, in some instances, required them to defray a part of the costs of construction. (*Cf.* Sax. "*Transport-und Kommunikationswesen*," in Schönberg's *Handbuch*, Vol. i., p. 546.)

CHAPTER X.

THE METHODS EMPLOYED BY THE UNITED STATES TO IMPROVE AND EXTEND INLAND WATERWAYS.

THE RIVER AND HARBOR BILL.

The work of improving and extending the inland waterways of the United States has been an enterprise of individuals, of the States, and of the Federal Government. The States preceded the general government in the field, and for obvious reasons. In the days preceding the advent of the railroad, when waterways were the chief means of communication, the State, as compared with the national government, stood relatively for more than it does to-day. Our Union of States was smaller, the powers exercised at Washington fewer. Our sense of nationality developed slowly. Promoters of inland commerce looked to Congress for aid but were generally obliged to fall back upon the States. There was an economic reason however, stronger than this political one. Commerce was then more local and less interstate in character. We now regard the United States, or are at least coming to do so, as the industrial and commercial unit; the great manufacturing centres of the East, and the agricultural regions of the West depend each on the other, and commerce knows no State boundaries. Transportation has now become very largely an interstate matter, but in the early decades of this century the future was fully realized. The States not only executed works of local significance, but Congress left them to construct waterways of such distinctively national importance as the Erie and the Illinois and Michigan Canals. New York, Illinois and Ohio are the only States now owning and operating canals.* Those other States which formerly owned canals have as was seen either sold them to corporations, abandoned them, or turned them over to the United

---

* For a history of canals, see Vol. IV. of Tenth Census of United States.

States. The improvement and extension of important waterways have become the charge of the nation; most local canals have passed out of the hands of the State into the ownership of corporations. The causes of this were noted in a previous connection.

The number of waterways which in the future receive aid from the United States needs in no case to be large. Purely local works should be local or individual enterprises, and those of interstate importance be carried on by the Federal Government. Congress has recently assumed charge of certain works of interstate importance that the States have been prosecuting. The Saint Mary's Canal and the Hudson River are instances of this. The discussion in Chapter VIII. was to the effect that individuals, the States and the National Government ought to co-operate in making improvements.

The action on the part of Congress in assuming charge of interstate commerce is one of the many indications of that development of the central government which is necessarily attending the expansion of our institutions over a new and large territory, the rapid growth in our population, and the fast increasing complexity of our industrial and social life. Inland navigation was naturally the part of interstate commerce of which Congress first assumed control. The natural waterways of most countries have been regarded as public ways since feudal times. They are now usually free highways. There were, therefore, historical reasons why the natural interstate water routes should be improved by Congress as soon as the growth in the population and industry of the United States made urgent the need for commerce. From 1789 Congress constructed the lighthouses, beacons, buoys, etc., necessary to render coastwise and lake commerce safer. In 1822 the Federal Government took out of the hands of the States the entire work of improving harbors, and began also to appropriate money to improve inland navigation. For ten years the Federal

Government, as well as the States, was active in works of internal improvement. Then came the dominance of strict constructionism, and the opposition of President Jackson and the Democrats to internal improvements. The Federal Government turned over canal building and most river improvements to the States. From Jackson's administration to the close of the war of the rebellion very little was done by Congress to foster inland navigation.*

The river and harbor bill in its present form dates from 1870. From 1830 to 1870 most appropriations for rivers and harbors were not made directly, but by means of riders attached to other bills.† The bill originates in the House Committee on Rivers and Harbors, and, since 1882, has

---

* The overthrow of the Whig system of internal improvements was not the result of political causes alone. Compare the author's paper on River and Harbor Bills in Volume II. of the ANNALS OF THE AMERICAN ACADEMY OF POLITICAL AND SOCIAL SCIENCE, May, 1892:

"The real causes of the abandonment of Congressional aid to road and canal building lay neither with President Jackson nor with strict construction. The building of turnpikes practically ceased with the advent of the railroad in 1830. The causes that led to the cessation of canal building were, first, the opposition to the tariff. The bitter struggle against the tariff of 1828 naturally included opposition to internal improvements—the other half of the American system. The second cause—a somewhat complex one—is found in the land policy of the United States. The large revenues from the tariff, and more especially from the land sales, caused a treasury surplus to exist during the years from 1830 to 1836; this surplus led to distribution, and distribution did much to put an end to internal improvements by the federal government. This large surplus could not be lessened by altering the tariff, because of the compromise of 1833; and the opposition to cheap lands was so strong that no measure decreasing the price of lands could be passed. In view of the existence of this surplus, and in view of Jackson's opposition to Congressional aid to local works of improvement, the Whigs changed front in the midst of the battle. They began advocating the distribution of the surplus arising from land sales among the States, and the surrender to the States of the prosecution of works of internal improvement. President Jackson had favored this plan in 1829, and afterward also; but in 1836 he abandoned distribution. The Whigs then very naturally clung to the idea all the more tenaciously. Distribution came in 1836, and with results so disastrous that there was soon no money to distribute. The odium attaching to distribution did much to bring into disrepute internal improvements, to foster which works the national funds had left the treasury. The third cause for the overthrow of the canal, and the strongest one, was the railroad. The extension of railroads during the decade from 1830 to 1840 was rapid, and the superiority which they possess over canals as agents of most kinds of traffic was quickly recognized."

† From 1854 to 1870 most appropriations were made under the head of "fortifications, etc."

been passed bi-ennially. The construction of the works provided for by the bill is in the charge of the Secretary of War and the United States engineers. Appropriations made on the basis of the surveys and estimates of the War Department are granted for works previously begun and for new ones. Each bill directs a large number of new surveys to be made * and the engineers make a report on the work either as "worthy" or as "unworthy" of execution. By "worthy of improvement" † the engineers mean that the project is feasible and that the increase of commerce which would result from the work would be sufficient to warrant the requisite outlay of capital. In declaring a waterway worthy of improvement, the engineers do not necessarily recommend the execution of the work. This fact is sometimes disregarded. The chief of engineers is required by law to make the estimates, but were he to name the works that Congress ought to undertake, he would recommend far fewer than Congress now authorizes.

The estimates submitted by the chief of engineers are for the costs necessary to complete each improvement, but if Congress authorizes the work it usually makes an appropriation only sufficient to begin the execution, often a sum only twenty-five per cent of the estimated expense of completion. This has been well styled the "driblet system of appropriations."‡

* The last bill, approved July 13, 1892, provided for 144.
† Section 7 of the last law reads as follows: "That the preliminary examinations ordered in this Act shall be made by the local engineer in charge of the district, or an engineer detailed for the purpose; and such local or detailed engineer and the division engineer of the locality shall report to the chief of engineers; first, whether, in their opinion, the harbor or river under such examination is worthy of improvement by the general government, and shall state in such report fully and particularly the facts and reasons on which they base such opinion, including the present and prospective demands of commerce, and, second, if worthy of improvement by the general government, what it will cost to survey the same, with the view of submitting plan and estimate for its improvement; and the chief of engineers shall submit to the Secretary of War the reports of the local and division engineers, with his views thereon and his opinion of the public necessity or convenience to be subserved by the proposed improvement, and all such reports of preliminary examinations with such recommendations as he may see proper to make, shall be submitted by the Secretary of War to the House of Representatives, and are hereby ordered to be printed when so made."
‡ Report of the House Committee on Rivers and Harbors, April 9, 1892.

The method by which Congress legislates may be illustrated by describing the framing of the bill of July 13, 1892. The purpose of the committee was to frame a twenty-one million dollar bill, that sum being what the condition of the treasury warranted. This general limit having been set, the estimates submitted by the chief of engineers were gone through with. The estimates of the amounts that might profitably be spent on works already begun were first considered, then those for new works were taken up. The former were greatly scaled down, and seventy of the new projects, of which the bill of 1890 had directed preliminary examination to be made and which had been reported by the engineers as "worthy," were excluded from consideration by the committee. As reported to the House the bill appropriated $21,209,975, and was based on estimates aggregating $69,814,915.* The bill contained 400 appropriations, of which only twenty-eight were for new works. The sum designated for the improvement of rivers and other waterway channels was $14,365,979; the sum for harbors, $6,799,996; for examinations, contingencies and incidental expenses, $125,000. As passed by the House the bill appropriated $21,346,975. The Senate Committee on Commerce raised the amount to $22,470,118. The sum that was finally appropriated was somewhat less than this.

* Compare the following itemized estimate taken the report of the House Committee on Rivers and Harbors:

Estimates of the chief of engineers of the amounts that can be profitably expended in the fiscal year ending June 30, 1893, exclusive of the Mississippi and Missouri rivers,	$52,489,950
Estimates of the Mississippi River Commission, including certain harbors on the river and for the work at the mouth of Red River,	7,275,000
Estimates of the Missouri River Commission,	3,100,000
Total for the old projects,	$62,864,950
Estimates of new projects considered by the committee for which appropriations have been recommended, but which are not included in the [above] estimates of the chief of engineers,†	6,949,995
Total for old projects and new projects considered by the committee,	$69,814,955

†This does not imply that the committee considered works which the engineers had not surveyed and submitted estimates concerning.

The execution of the works of improvement for which appropriations are thus made is let to contractors by the Secretary of War. He and the United States engineers have control over the work done by the contractors.

Our method of aiding the improvement of inland navigation differs from those pursued by England, Germany and France, and a glance at their methods will prepare the way to a more intelligent criticism of our legislation. In England most improvements of rivers and harbors have been made at the expense of corporations, municipal and private. The execution of the works is performed sometimes by a municipality, but usually by a "trust;" i. e., a private corporation chartered by Parliament. These trusts often are aided by cities and by Parliament, and collect harbor dues and tolls. In Germany, as might be expected from the nature of the State, the government takes the initiative, pays for the works and executes them herself. In France, also, the State defrays the expense of improving and extending inland navigation. The Department of Public Works has charge of the improvement of inland navigation ; it submits plans and estimates for the works needed on rivers, canals and harbors. The plans and estimates, however, unlike those submitted by the United States chief of engineers, are submitted largely on the department's own initiative, and are made with the end in view of securing for the country as a whole a unified system of inland water routes. The execution of the works that are authorized is sometimes carried out directly by the government, whose engineers employ the laborers and supervise their work, often by contractors, according to the plans and under the supervision of the engineers of the Department of Public Works.

The distinguishing feature of the English as contrasted with our method of improving inland navigation is the essentially private character of the former. The method followed by France and the German States differs from that pursued by the United States, first, in the systematic character of the former as opposed to the local, sporadic nature of ours; second, in the greater power given the administrative branch of government as regards both the initiation of works of improvement and the exercise of discretion in the expenditure of money appropriated; and, third, in the fact that the French and Germans consider plans for making a particular improvement *in toto*. The legislature considers plans, as, indeed, we do, for the entire, the completed work; but, unlike us, if they decide to make an improvement they appropriate money enough to enable the entire enterprise to be begun and contracts made for the execution of the whole work.

These differences between our own method of making improvements and those of other countries suggest several criticisms of the River and Harbor Bill. As regards the improvement of important inland waterways by the State and by corporations, the arguments in favor of the State are conclusive. They were given in Chapter VIII., and need not be repeated here. Our policy in this regard is decidedly preferable to that of England. In another regard both England and the United States have failed to secure the best results from the improvement of inland water routes. Neither country has anything like a system of inland waterways, constructed according to one common standard of dimensions. Although still far from completing the task, France has done much to bring about unity in her system of inland waterways. In the United States, on the contrary, the sporadic character of our works has prevented the unification of our natural inland water routes. Although the United States has spent nearly $230,000,000 on rivers and harbors during this century, the commerce of the Great Lakes is still practically unconnected with the sea and with the great river system of the Mississippi Valley, while the commerce of the Pacific slope is still waiting for access to the Mississippi and the Atlantic by way of a Nicaragua Canal. It has been seen in a previous chapter how rapidly the inland commerce of

France has increased since the government has begun the reconstruction of her waterways with the intent of giving them common dimensions. The passage of freight from one water-course to another without reloading is essential to an extensive inland navigation. Reloading causes delay, and adds heavily to costs of transportation. There has been such a decrease in the expense of traction that the costs of loading and unloading have become a proportionally larger item of expense than formerly. Many kinds of bulky freight cannot bear the costs of reloading so easily as a higher tariff by rail.

Again, our plan results in the execution of too many works. The bill of 1890 made appropriations for 435 works. Think of it, 435 works to be carried on by means of a bi-ennial appropriation of $25,000,000 ! There are 400 items in the bill of 1892. The chief of engineers has often opposed this policy, and urged Congress to undertake fewer works; but the pressure of Congressmen is steadily stronger for more works.* The bill of 1892 provided for 144 new surveys, and that of 1890 for 203. More than half of these 203 proposed works were declared "unworthy of improvement," and of those declared worthy only a few would have been recommended by the chief of engineers. The House Committee, as was said above, recommended appropriations for twenty-eight new works and that was doubtless too many.

The practice of log-rolling is in large degree responsible for the great number of appropriations for rivers and harbors. Log-rolling has so often been inveighed against that no further invectives are in place here; indeed, more sins have already been charged up to the practice than it is answerable for. Less money is doubtless expended on works of purely

---

* Compare this with the following statement by the House Committee on Rivers and Harbors, which framed the bill of 1892 : The pressure for river and harbor appropriations was never before as great as that which the committee encountered in the preparation of the bill reported, and if the committee had yielded to half of the demands, many of which were urged with great force and earnestness, the bill would have carried many millions more than it now does.

local benefit, as a result of log-rolling, than is generally claimed;* it is, however, a most undesirable way of legislating and one we shall find hard to avoid in regard to river and harbor appropriations as long as we continue the present plan of looking to the representatives in Congress instead of to the administrative branch of the government, as the real initiative in recommending such works of improvement; at least as long as the representatives continue to subordinate national improvements of greater commercial importance to local ones of lesser significance, so long will log-rolling continue. The cure consists in freeing representatives from the pressure at present exerted on them to work for improvements in their own districts whatever be the relative need of the same. This will be most quickly and surely secured by holding the administrative branch of the government to a higher degree of responsibility, and by giving it greater power, in regard to the improvement of inland navigation. The Secretary of War, through the chief of engineers, should have greater influence, by means of reports and personal attendance on the sessions of the committees that frame the bill, in shaping legislation. Furthermore, the Secretary of War ought to have greater discretionary power as to the way in which the money appropriated shall be applied. When President Arthur vetoed the river and harbor bill of 1882, he recommended that Congress authorize the Secretary of War and the President to spend such of the money appropriated as they thought best, the restriction being imposed on them that they should spend money only on the objects named in the bill, and that they should spend no more on a particular work than the bill authorized. Whether in detail or not, in principle at least, this recommendation to vest the Secretary of War with greater discretionary power in the outlay of money which has been appropriated was sound. The Secretary of War, aided by the counsel of the United States engineers, is better able than Congress to apply the money

* For a justification of this statement see the author's "River and Harbor Bills."

granted scientifically and economically to an improvement. He is practically free from local influence, is subjected to but little political pressure, his only object can be the wisest administration of his department. The democratic spirit of Americans is chary of granting much power to the executive. The French have secured great advantages from giving the executive branch of the government extensive powers over inland navigation. To a large extent the administrative part of our government is still undeveloped, and the small discretionary power given the Secretary of War over the application of money appropriated to improve rivers and harbors is but one instance of the fact.

The most objectionable feature of our river and harbor legislation is our driblet system of appropriations. This plan encourages the commencement of more works than would otherwise be begun. Congress feels freer to authorize a work when the immediate appropriation is small. The brunt of the burden is thus not only shifted onto future legislators, but becomes greater by virtue of the shifting. River and harbor improvements are often begun and left for sometime in an unfinished state. This causes a great waste of capital, adding, in some cases, from twenty-five to fifty per cent to the cost.* Driblet appropriations cause another waste by compelling engineers to adopt unscientific plans in executing the works. Many engineering projects require plans reaching through a series of years in order to secure satisfactory results. Furthermore, the present way of making appropriations often precludes large contracts thus adding materially to final costs. Lastly the works thus constructed at increased costs begin to be useful to the public at a later date. The investment does not yield returns so soon and thus becomes so much less profitable.

These objections to partial appropriations are realized by Congress, and a very commendable step has been taken to modify our way of making grants and to improve on old

* See report of Senate Committee on Commerce, May 13, 1892.

methods. The framers of the bill of 1890 tried an experiment. Without actually adopting the French and German plan of appropriating at once, or making available a sum sufficient to enable contracts to be made for the entire completion of a work, they hit upon a way of reaching the same result. The limited amount which could be taken at once from the Treasury for rivers and harbors prevented making lump appropriations for works; so, in the case of five important improvements—St. Mary's Falls Canal, the Hay Lake Channel, Michigan; the harbors of Philadelphia, Baltimore, and Galveston—it was provided " That such contracts as may be desirable may be entered into by the Secretary of War for the completion of the existing project, or any part of the same, to be paid for as appropriations may from time to time be made by law." The result was a saving of from ten to sixty-seven per cent of the original estimates by means of continuing contracts. General Casey, chief of engineers, calculated the amount saved to be $5,000,000. The experiment was so successful that the principal was applied to the twelve most important items of the bill of July 13, 1892. The Secretary of War is authorized to make contracts for the completion of the following improvements: Harbor of Refuge, Point Judith, R. I.; Charleston Harbor, S. C.; Savannah Harbor, Ga.; Mobile Harbor, Ala.; Humboldt Harbor, Cal.; Hudson River, N. Y.; Ship Channel, Great Lakes; canal at Cascades of Columbia River, Ore.; mouth of St. John's River, Fla.; Great Kanawha River, W. Va. In the case of the improvements of the Missouri River and the Upper and Lower Mississippi, the appropriation of a definite amount per year for three years beginning July 1, 1893, makes possible continuous and systematic improvements. Three of this list of twelve were added to the bill by the Senate, the Lower Missouri River, mouth of St. John's River and Great Kanawha River. The amount granted by the bill for these twelve works is $6,632,500, or about thirty per cent of the total appropriated, and an additional maximum sum of $31,755,521 is authorized by the bill for the completion of the work, or continuance as in the case of the Missouri and Mississippi Rivers, during the next three years. The saving because of this partial change in our policy of making appropriations will surely be large. We should adopt this way of appropriating for all works. The House Committee, which framed the bill of 1892, was of the opinion that "had this policy been adopted a dozen years ago, it would have resulted in a saving to the government in the matter of river and harbor improvements of $20,000,000, out of the aggregate appropriated in that time for such work."

The River and Harbor Bill has, on the whole, been more harshly criticised than it has deserved. It is true that the United States is carrying on too many works; that logrolling plays too great a rôle in legislation; that the influence of the United States engineers and the Secretary of War in deciding what works shall be begun, and how and where the money appropriated shall be applied, is too small; and that our methods are often unscientific and wasteful; still, the changes inaugurated by the last two bills are important, and contain the promise of further progress. The importance of our inland navigation is coming home to us more and more, and the demand of the future will not be for less expenditure, but for greater; and we may confidently expect these increased appropriations to go in a more scientific way to a smaller number of works.

CHAPTER XI.

THE LEADING WORKS IN PROCESS OF EXECUTION WITHIN THE UNITED STATES. PROPOSED WORKS.

The United States is pursuing a liberal policy in the development of her inland waterways. The preceding reference to the River and Harbor Bill shows that this liberality results in the simultaneous execution of a large—indeed, too large—number of works. The desirability of concentration of effort upon the more important improvements has been emphasized. Of these larger inland commercial routes of the United States, the Mississippi River, the Great Lakes, the waterways by which they have been and are to be connected and extended and the Nicaragua Canal, by which the east and the west shall be joined, rank first.

The improvement of the Mississippi River is under the charge of the Mississippi River Commission, organized by Act of Congress, June 28, 1879, and consisting of seven members, four of whom are United States engineers and three civilians. The importance of the river to transportation is further recognized by Congress by the establishment of standing committees to look after its needs. The House Committee on Levees and Improvement of the Mississippi River and the Senate Committee on Improvement of the Mississippi River and its Tributaries have charge of legislation concerning the river. With the improvement of the mouth of the Mississippi by means of the jetties which Captain Eads successfully completed in 1879 every one is more or less familiar. The works of improvement at present consist mainly in the construction of reservoirs at the head waters to secure water for release during the season when the river is lowest, in the construction of wing dams to confine the channel and cause it to maintain a greater depth, and in dredging the channels and harbors of the river.

For this work the River and Harbor Bill of 1892 appropriated $3,655,000 to be expended on the Mississippi River, exclusive of its branches. Of its tributaries, the Ohio, Cumberland, Tennessee and Kentucky rivers alone received $1,525,000. The bill also authorizes contracts to be entered into by the Mississippi River Commission that may entail a maximum expenditure of $12,870,000 during the next three years.

The improvement of the Missouri River is likewise under the supervision of a commission. This body consists of three army engineers and two civilians. The commission is improving the river in a systematic way by completing the work on one reach after another, beginning with the mouth of the stream and working up. The bill of 1892 appropriates $752,500, and authorizes contracts involving the expenditure of $2,225,000 during the three years from 1893 to 1896.

The most important item in the bill of 1892 is the appropriation for the construction of "a ship channel, twenty and twenty-one feet in depth, and a minimum width of three hundred feet in the shallows of the connecting waters of the Great Lakes between Chicago, Duluth and Buffalo." The total cost of the work is estimated at $3,340,000, and the bill authorizes the United States engineers to enter into contracts for completing the entire work. As a result of the urgent demands of the commercial interests of the West, Congress provided in the bill of 1890 for the examination of the channels connecting the lakes. In the report of the survey by Colonel O. M. Poe, who is the engineer in charge of the improvements of the Great Lakes, the feasibility and desirability of the work were strongly set forth. The men most interested in the commerce of the lakes met in convention at Detroit, December 17 and 18, 1891, and sent a memorial to Congress urging it to authorize the work and to make the necessary appropriation. The result was the clause in the bill of 1892, to which reference has been made. The work of improving the harbors of the Great Lakes is being adequately cared for by liberal appropriations of Congress.

In view of the zeal Congress is manifesting in the improvement of the Great Lakes and the Mississippi River, it is surprising to find that the work of connecting and co-ordinating these two great systems of inland waterways has not been correspondingly pushed. The fullest use of the natural waterways cannot be possible as long as they are connected by such an inefficient canal as the Illinois and Michigan, extending from Chicago to La Salle on the Illinois River. At present Lake Michigan is connected with the Mississippi River by this canal and the improved Illinois River. Congress is now carrying on the work which the State of Illinois had previously begun, of canalizing the Illinois River. "The ultimate object of this improvement is to furnish a through route of transportation by water from the southern end of Lake Michigan to the Mississippi River of sufficient capacity for its navigation by the largest class of Mississippi River steamboats that can reach the mouth of the Illinois River."* The United States has also begun the construction of the Illinois and Mississippi (the so-called Hennepin) Canal from the great bend of the Illinois River near the town of Hennepin to the mouth of Rock River. This canal is to be ninety-seven miles long, eighty feet wide, seven feet deep, and with locks 170 feet long, with thirty-five feet in width of lock chamber, and is, of course, to be constructed so that river steamers can navigate it. This canal will shorten the water route from Chicago to all points north of the mouth of the Rock River by 419 miles, will surely increase the traffic on the upper Mississippi and exercise an important influence as regulator of the freight charges in the Upper Mississippi Valley; that is, will do so as soon as the Illinois and Michigan Canal has also been reconstructed. That is at present a barge canal six feet

* Report of Committee on Commerce, U. S. Senate. Report No. 666, Fifty-second Congress, first session, p. 375.

deep and sixty feet wide, on which there is a traffic of but 1,500,000 tons annually. Boats of the size that can pass the locks of the Illinois River must at present stop at La Salle and transfer their cargo to the smaller boats of the Illinois and Michigan Canal. It is to be hoped that the enlargement of this waterway will not be long delayed,* and that the Illinois and Mississippi Canal will be put through as soon as possible.

In speaking of the improvement of the waterways of the Mississippi Valley, the Ohio River and its branches, the Kentucky, the Cumberland and the Tennessee deserve especial notice. The large amount of traffic on the Ohio has already been referred to.† Nearly eight million dollars have been expended on the river since 1827, when the first works were begun. The Ohio is 967 miles long, and is at present navigable throughout its entire length for coal boats drawing six feet of water. This, however, is possible for only 155 days of each year on the average. The proposed improvements would make this coal traffic possible from one to three months longer each year. Of course, the ordinary smaller-draft river boats can navigate the stream throughout the season of navigation. The last River and Harbor Bill appropriated $560,000 for use on the Ohio River.

The Kentucky, Cumberland and Tennessee rivers, like the Ohio River, flow from rich lumber and mineral regions through fertile agricultural districts. Steamboats navigate the Kentucky to Frankfort, and large amounts of freight are brought down the river from the Three Forks in flat boats. The tonnage on the Kentucky in 1891 was nearly 400,000 tons—double what it was eight years ago. The existing

---

* Or that the Chicago drainage canal, now being constructed to connect Chicago with the Illinois River, will be pushed to an early completion. This canal is to be fed by the waters of Lake Michigan, is to drain the sewage of Chicago into the Illinois River, and is to have dimensions that will make it navigable for lake and river boats.

† *Vide supra*, page 45.

project has for its object a slack-water navigation for boats of six feet draft. Up to 1890, $1,163,077 had been expended; $1,674,000 is the sum estimated as required to complete the work. The bill of 1892 appropriated only $150,000 for the purpose. The Cumberland River receives, in the bill of 1892, an appropriation of $290,000 for continuing its canalization. At present steamboats of three feet draft ascend the river to Point Burnside, Kentucky, from four to six months of the year. Steamboats drawing two and a half feet run to Carthage, 118 miles above Nashville, from six to eight months of the year. Below Nashville boats drawing sixteen inches can run the entire year. It will take nearly seven million dollars to make the stream navigable for larger river boats to the shoals of the river, 337 miles above Nashville. Should the work be carried out, the stream will surely become of large commercial importance.

The Tennessee River ranks among the largest of the forty-odd tributaries of the Mississippi. The stream presents several obstructions to navigation, but these have been partially overcome, so that the river is navigable for a distance of 650 miles from its mouth. On the 456 miles below Chattanooga $3,180,877 had been expended, previous to 1890, in blasting and dredging, and in constructing three canals, with a total length of twenty-four miles, to overcome the difficulties of navigating the shoals and rapids of the river. By the last River and Harbor Bill, $500,000 is appropriated for improvements below Chattanooga, and $25,000 for work above that city. For completing the work below Chattanooga, it is estimated that $5,565,762 will be required. The River and Harbor Bill of 1890 directed a survey to be made of the Upper Tennessee from Chattanooga to the junction of the Holston and French Broad rivers, a distance of 188 miles. It is estimated that a three-foot channel at low water can be secured by expending $650,000. There are at present fifty-two steamers plying the Tennessee. The traffic on the river is not large, but must certainly become so with the improvement of the stream and with the development of the mining, manufacturing and agricultural industries of the Tennessee Valley.

The Hudson River is receiving extensive improvements. This is, next to the Mississippi, the most important navigable river of the United States. It has a three-fold relation to commerce. For a hundred miles it is deep enough to float the large ocean ships, it has the largest local traffic of any river of its length in the United States, and forms, as well, a part of the system of inland waterways that terminate in New York.* The plan of improvement entered upon in 1867 provided for an eleven foot channel from New Baltimore to Albany, and a nine foot one from Albany to Troy. Commerce outgrew these dimensions, and the River and Harbor Bill of 1890 provided for the appointment of a board of engineers to examine and report on three projects : A channel from New York to Albany for sea-going vessels of twenty-foot draft, a channel of like dimensions from New York to Troy, and a navigable channel of twelve feet depth at mean low water from New York to Troy. The board was of "the opinion that the possible benefits to commerce to be derived from the proposed improvement for vessels drawing twenty feet are not under existing conditions, sufficient to justify at this time the expenditure necessary to make such improvement," but "that the third project contained in the act of September 19, 1890, which provides for improving the Hudson River 'between Coxsackie and the State dam at Troy to such an extent as to secure a navigable channel twelve feet deep at mean low water' is a worthy and useful one." The estimated cost of the work is $2,447,000 ; and the bill of 1893 authorizes the work, makes an appropriation of $187,500 to begin its execution, and provides for making contracts for the entire project to be paid for from time to time by succeeding appropriations.

Another important work of river improvement upon which

* Cf. Statistics of tonnage, page 8.

the United States has entered is the canalization of the Columbia River. By overcoming the obstruction to navigation presented at the Cascades, 160 miles from the ocean and at the Dalles, 220 miles from the sea, the Columbia River can easily be made navigable for large river steamers through a distance of 1032 miles, of which 752 are in the United States. Its tributaries, the Williamette, the Snake and other rivers, can be made to add 600 miles more of navigation. The Columbia may justly be regarded as the Mississippi of the West.* The bar at the mouth of the river has just been removed by the construction of a jetty that secures a channel thirty feet deep. The lower Columbia and the Williamette, below Portland, now have channels twenty feet deep, and the River and Harbor Bill of 1892 appropriates $150,000 to be applied to obtain a twenty-five foot channel. It will not be long before the large-sized ocean ships will unload their cargoes at the docks of Portland, 110 miles from the sea. The Cascades of the Columbia are about four and a half miles in length, the river having a fall of forty-five feet at high water. The

---

* Very few people living in the Mississippi Valley and the Eastern States have any adequate conception of the extent and fertility of the region drained by the Columbia River system. The following sentences taken from the report of the Senate Committee on Transportation Routes to the Sea, submitted February 8, 1892, are instructive: "The Columbia River and its tributaries drain a region of country unsurpassed, if indeed equaled, in agricultural, grazing and mineral productiveness by any area of equal size on the habitable globe; a region, in so far as it relates to its agricultural aspects, susceptible of the highest degree of cultivation, and of producing crops of cereals, especially wheat, unprecedented in both quantity and quality by the product of the most highly cultivated fields of the choicest cereal producing lands in the civilized world, while its facilities for grazing and fruit growing, its timber, mineral resources of gold, silver, lead, coal, and other valuable minerals can scarcely be properly or accurately described without seeming exaggeration.

"Nor is this area by any means insignificant in geographical extent. It is equal in extent to over one-fifteenth of the entire area of the United States: over one-fourth of the aggregate areas of all the republics of South America ; larger than all of the six New England States, with all the Middle States and Maryland, Virginia and West Virginia thrown in. It is twice the size of Great Britain and Ireland.

"The Columbia River drains an area of about 345,355 square miles. The Snake River alone, the principal tributary flowing into it over three hundred miles from the sea, drains an area of 105,000 square miles."

obstruction to navigation is being overcome by the construction of a lock and a canal 3000 feet long. The River and Harbor Bill of 1892, authorized contracts for its completion at a further cost not to exceed $1,745,000. The obstructions at the Dalles are nearly twelve miles long and the entire fall of the river in this distance is eighty-one and a half feet at low water. The expenses of overcoming these difficulties will necessarily be large. By the River and Harbor Act of 1888, the Secretary of War was directed to appoint a board of three engineers from the United States army to report on the best method of improving the river. The board was of opinion that a canal with locks would cost more than the commerce of the river warranted, and reported in favor of the construction of two hydraulic lifts, one near the lower end of the Dalles and one near the upper end. The boats were to be conveyed from one lift to the other by means of a boat railway eight miles long. The lifts and railway were to be large enough to handle boats 165 feet long, with thirty-eight feet beam, and five feet draft, and weighing, together with cargo, 600 tons. The estimated cost of structure and equipment for passing eight boats each way in twelve hours was $2,860,356.55, and at an added outlay of $716,000, forty boats could be passed each way in twenty-four hours. The plan was not, however, accepted by Congress, and the River and Harbor Bill of 1892 authorizes the President to appoint a board of engineers to consist of seven members, three of whom shall be civilians, to re-examine the obstruction to navigation at the Dalles and to report on the best method of overcoming them.

One of the principal canal constructions now in process of execution is the enlargement of the Chesapeake and Delaware Canal into a waterway for ocean ships. This work is being carried on by a private company and not by the government.

These are some of the more important works now being executed, besides them are several proposed works of which mention ought to be made. As is to be expected the larger works that are being discussed are those whose purpose is to extend the greatest of all natural inland waterways, the Great Lakes. Probably one of the first lake-ship canals constructed will connect Pittsburgh with Lake Erie. Pittsburgh and the neighboring district now does an annual business with the lakes to the extent of about 5,000,000 tons of iron ore and 2,000,000 tons of coal.* The industries about the Great Lakes obtain most of their coal from Pennsylvania. At present this is shipped to the lake by rail and then transferred to boats. In 1889 the State of Pennsylvania appointed a commission to report on the feasibility of a ship canal. It reported such a work to be possible of construction, and suggested a waterway by way of the Beaver River, to be 103 miles long, 152 feet wide at the surface and 15 feet deep, with 50 locks, 300 feet long by 45 feet in width. The estimated cost is $27,000,000. The Senate of the United States passed a bill authorizing a survey to be made of a canal route from the lake to Pittsburgh, but the bill failed in the House. Should such a waterway be put through, and Pittsburgh will hardly rest content till she becomes a lake port, it is probable that the canal will be given greater depth than fifteen feet and be constructed with less than fifty locks.

Mention was made on page 13 of the formation of the Minnesota Canal Company for the purpose of constructing a waterway from St. Paul and Minneapolis to Lake Superior. The desire for cheaper coal is the chief reason for the formation of the company. At present the freight per ton of anthracite coal from Buffalo is $1.80, with a lake-ship canal to St. Paul and Minneapolis the rate can be reduced to eighty cents. The millers of Minneapolis and the farmers of Minnesota and the Dakotas would be greatly benefited by the extension of lake commerce to these important manufacturing and distributing centres.

* *Cf.* Report by Roberts on "Uses of Waterways and Railways," to Fifth International Congress on Inland Navigation.

WORKS IN PROCESS OF EXECUTION. 131

The connection of the Great Lakes with the ocean is a work that has, very naturally, been frequently considered as the commerce on the Great Lakes has developed. A lake and ocean-ship waterway between the Great Lakes and the ocean is a natural sequence of the twenty-foot channel for the lakes. Canada is now actively improving the St. Lawrence and Welland canal route, and giving them the depth of fourteen feet. When this work was begun that was the draft of lake vessels, but in the future they are to draw twenty feet. The costs of a deep canal through the United States are unknown, no surveys have been made. Until that has been done, it will be impossible to discuss the subject intelligently. All admit the great importance which a deep-water channel to the sea would have. The commerce of the Great Lakes is enormous, and would be greatly increased by having outlet to the sea.

There has been a good deal of discussion whether the deep-water channel to the sea should pass by way of the St. Lawrence River or from the lakes to New York City; but the question seems clearly to have but one answer as far as the United States is concerned. However desirable it may be for Canada to have deep-water communication between her western territory and Quebec, Montreal and her other eastern cities, and however important it may be for Canada to have a water route from Canadian fields, forests, mines and shops to Liverpool and other markets of Europe, the case with us still remains different. Our concern is primarily to connect the Great Lakes with the great cities of the eastern States. They are our chief markets, trade with England is desirable, but it has only a secondary importance. The traffic on the Welland Canal is comparatively light; in 1890 it was only 960,020 tons, or about one-third that on the smaller, essentially barge-traffic, Erie canal. The St. Lawrence route would not only have less commercial value for us, but it would increase rather than lessen our commercial and industrial dependence. Our political relations with Canada and

England would be injured by such a waterway. We should have about 1400 miles of coast line from which our ocean cruisers and men-of-war could be excluded. As long as Canada remains a dependency of Great Britain, our commercial and political interests will remain opposed to hers.

Two other canal projects have been mooted not a little—the construction of a waterway for lake ships and river boats between Cincinnati and Lake Erie, and an ocean-ship canal between Philadelphia and New York City. A bill was passed by the Senate of the Fifty-second Congress directing surveys of these routes to be made, but the bill did not get through the House. Concerning the importance which the canal between America's great commercial city and her greatest manufacturing city would have, there can be no doubt. Such a waterway will doubtless be constructed in the not distant future, either by the government or, as is more probable, by private capital.

The greatest of all canals now in process of construction, whether domestic or foreign trade be considered, is the Nicaragua. Its importance makes it merit a separate chapter.

CHAPTER XII.
THE NICARAGUA CANAL.

The Nicaragua Canal is as much an inland waterway of the United States, as regards a large part of the commercial service it will perform, as it would be were it to extend across the country from New York to San Francisco. Its function as an agent of domestic commerce is to connect the Pacific Slope with the Gulf States, the Mississippi Valley, and the Atlantic States. It connects the rivers of the Valley of the Columbia with the Mississippi system just as truly as the canals across Illinois are to furnish an efficient waterway from the Mississippi to the Great Lakes. As the commerce of the Mississippi will be increased by this water route from Chicago to La Salle and Rock Island, so to a large degree does the commercial usefulness of the Mississippi and Columbia systems depend on the Nicaragua Canal. The waterway will be an equally important route for the movement of our coast-wise traffic, as distinct from the strictly inland traffic; it will be, as President Hayes said, "virtually a part of the coast line of the United States." Besides this it will become an important highway for the foreign commerce of our own country and of the other nations of the world. It will, then, be a waterway performing the three-fold functions of a route for inland, coastwise and foreign commerce, and these functions determine how the canal should be controlled and administered. The first two of these decide that the United States should control the waterway, the third that the United States in controlling the administration of the canal must maintain the neutrality of the waterway for the "impartial and innocent use" of all nations.

Whoever constructs the Nicaragua Canal, be it the United States directly or a company chartered by our own or some other government, the United States must control the waterway. Our commercial interests in the canal are so much greater than those of any other nation that it would be prejudicial to our welfare to allow any other State to dominate this artery of commerce. Military considerations are hardly inferior to commercial, and emphasize not only the necessity for the construction of the canal but also the reason why the waterway should be under American control. Without the canal our Pacific coast is separated from our Atlantic seaboard by nearly 15,000 miles, and in order to protect both sides of our country from attack we have to maintain a fleet on each ocean. With a canal, but under control of a foreign nation, our military position would be essentially the same. *

There is nothing in our present treaty relations with foreign powers to prevent us from controlling the Nicaragua Canal. Whoever constructs the canal, some great power must assure its neutrality; Nicaragua and Costa Rica are too weak to do this; the superiority at present of our interests in the waterway makes us the natural beneficiary of this right to maintain the canal as a neutral highway. By our treaties there is nothing to prevent the United States from aiding a corporation to build the canal; but, more than this, the United States to-day clearly has the right to negotiate with Nicaragua and Costa Rica for the purpose of obtaining for herself a right of way through Nicaragua, and the privilege of constructing the waterway directly without the intervention of a corporation.† In other words, the Clayton-Bulwer Treaty of 1850 is defunct.

* *Cf.* President Hayes' message to Congress, March 8, 1880: "An interoceanic canal across the isthmus will essentially change the geographical relations between the Atlantic and Pacific coasts of the United States, and between the United States and the rest of the world. It will be the great ocean thoroughfare between our Atlantic and Pacific shores, and virtually a part of the coast line of the United States. Our mere commercial interest in it is greater than that of all other countries, while its relation to our power and prosperity as a nation, to our means of defence, our unity, peace, and safety, are matters of paramount concern to the people of the United States. No other great power would, under similiar circumstances, fail to assert a rightful control over a work so closely and vitally affecting its interest and welfare."

† It would be foreign to the essentially economic purpose of this monograph to go more than briefly into this question. The argument is merely outlined. For a fuller discussion of the matter, consult the report of the Senate Committee on Foreign Relations, No. 1944, Fifty-first Congress, second session; also, speech by Senator Frye, *Congressional Record*, Fifty-second Congress, second session, vol. xxiv, p. 1630; and speech by Senator Morgan, same volume, p. 1685.

By the Clayton-Bulwer Treaty, England and the United States expressed "their views and intentions with reference to any means of communication by ship canal" across the isthmus.* The treaty was called forth by our acquisition of a large territory from Mexico just before 1850, and by the discovery of gold in the newly-acquired territory. A canal across the isthmus was much discussed, and seemed about to be realized in the near future. By the convention it was agreed that neither nation should ever obtain exclusive control over the canal, or "colonize or assume or exercise any domain over Nicaragua, Costa Rica, the Mosquito Coast, *or any part of Central America.*" It provided against there being any time lost in commencing the construction of the canal; either nation might give its support and encouragement to any persons of sufficient capital who might offer to undertake the work; the two nations were to defend the neutrality of the canal, the privilege being reserved of withdrawing such guaranty on notice.

"The convention of 1850 has become obsolete,"† and for several reasons. In the first place, the contracting parties looked forward to the immediate construction of the canal, but forty-three years have now passed and the only action that has been taken by either nation was the act of the United States Congress, in 1889, chartering the Maritime Canal Company of Nicaragua. During this time important political and economic events have put a new phase on the matter. England has not lived up to the agreements of the treaty. When the convention was made there existed a company of English subjects at Balize, Spanish territory, whom the Spanish government had licensed to cut timber. In 1853, this settlement of licensed wood-cutters organized a legislative assembly; in 1859, Great Britain negotiated a

---

* *Cf.* Rhodes: "History of the United States from the Compromise of 1850." Vol. i, pp. 199-202.

† Quoted from the report of the Senate Committee on Foreign Relations, January 10, 1890. John Sherman was the chairman of the committee, and George F. Edmunds and Wm. M. Evarts were two of the other members.

treaty with Guatemala to establish the boundaries between "Her Majesty's settlement and *possessions* in the Bay of Honduras" and the territories of Guatemala. Three years later England declared the settlement a colony and gave it a colonial government. All this was done by Great Britain after she had agreed not to "colonize or assume or exercise any dominion over . . . any part of Central America." The United States, in 1867, made a treaty with the republic of Nicaragua, in which the United States secured for its citizens the right of transit between the two oceans, in common with the citizens of Nicaragua, on any route that might be constructed. Nicaragua made a similar treaty with France and with England; but in 1884 we decided to take a further step. President Arthur negotiated a treaty with Nicaragua that gave the United States the suzerainty, though not absolute sovereignty, over a strip twelve miles wide through Nicaragua. The United States was to construct the canal, and was to defend the sovereignty of Nicaragua and to secure to the Central American States the benefits of the waterway. The treaty did not secure the necessary two-thirds majority of the Senate; but might have obtained it on reconsideration had not President Cleveland withdrawn the treaty because it was "coupled with absolute and unlimited engagements to defend the territorial integrity of the States where such interests lie." This treaty, of course, assumed that the Clayton-Bulwer convention had been abandoned by tacit consent of the contracting parties; and such is in reality the case. There has been no objection made by European powers to the efforts of the United States to promote the construction of the canal; England has not carried out the stipulations of the treaty, and the commercial and economic conditions have so changed since 1850 that the United States would not now think of agreeing to such a treaty as she then entered into. Since that time the Suez Canal has been put through and has passed under the control of England. England's commercial supremacy is secure against our competition, and will continue so until we find a shorter route to the western coast of South America and to the lands beyond the Pacific. But what has done most to change our attitude toward the Nicaragua Canal is the rapid development of the States on the Pacific. The imperative need of cheaper transportation between the eastern and western parts of the United States that arises from the differences in the industrial character of the two regions has made the Nicaragua Canal essentially a part of the inland transportation routes of the United States.

It is not our privilege alone, but our duty as well, to exercise political control over the Nicaragua Canal, both for the reason already given that we are the only nation of the Western Hemisphere that is strong enough to do this, and more because of the course which events have taken since 1885. The rejection of the treaty of 1884 was interpreted by the American promoters of the canal and by the Nicaraguan government as meaning that the United States did not intend to undertake the construction of the waterway; thus on the third of December, 1886, Messrs. Daly, Stout, Hotchkiss, Taylor, Billings, Crowninshield, Hitchcock, Miller and Menocal organized the Nicaragua Canal Association for the purpose of obtaining the concession of a right of way for the construction of a ship canal through Nicaragua. Mr. A. G. Menocal carried on the negotiations, and obtained the concessions, April 24, 1887. It was now necessary to find or establish a corporation to undertake the construction of the work; accordingly, the Nicaragua Canal Construction Company was incorporated June 10, 1887, under the laws of Colorado, with a capital fixed at $12,000,-000. Then on the twelfth of August, 1887, the Nicaragua Canal Association turned over to the Nicaragua Canal Construction Company, in consideration for $11,998,000 of the latter company's capital stock, the Nicaraguan concession and all the rights and property arising from its possession.

The association, however, retained the right to organize the Maritime Canal Company of Nicaragua in the future. The chief object of the association was to have the canal begun, thus it turned back into the treasury of the construction company, as a gift, six millions of the stock it had just received, and the construction company raised money by the sale of this stock to begin the work. Upon the arrival of the engineering party at Greytown, in Nicaragua, Costa Rica protested that the canal could not be constructed over the proposed route without her consent, because of the rights she possessed to the use of the port at Greytown and to the navigation of the San Juan River, which had been secured to her by the treaty of 1858 with Nicaragua. Nicaragua denied Costa Rica's claim; the question was arbitrated by President Cleveland, and decided in favor of Costa Rica. The Nicaragua Canal Association then obtained the necessary concession of right of way from Costa Rica, August 9, 1888, and turned this also over to the construction company. The following year, May 24, 1889, was when this transfer took place. Previous to this the United States Congress had passed an act, approved February 20, 1889, incorporating the Maritime Canal Company of Nicaragua, a body consisting essentially of the same men as composed the construction company, and having its headquarters in New York City. This company was the successor of the association; its president is Hiram Hotchkiss, of New York. On the twenty-fourth of May, 1889, the Nicaragua Canal Construction Company transferred to the Maritime Canal Company of Nicaragua, the two concessions given by Nicaragua and Costa Rica, together with the rights and property which their possession had conveyed, receiving as a remuneration $12,000,000 in full paid-up shares of the capital stock of the Maritime Canal Company. The construction company, of which ex-Senator Warner Miller is the president, then at once organized and sent out an expedition for beginning the work of construction. The party arrived at San Juan del Norte, or Greytown, June 3, 1889, and since then the work has gone more or less steadily onward.

These events have changed the political relations of the United States to the canal. The Maritime Canal Company of Nicaragua consists of American citizens; to this body of Americans Nicaragua and Costa Rica have granted the right to construct the interoceanic waterway; this company is chartered by the United States government, and in its stock Nicaragua and Costa Rica are each shareholders.

Surveys for the location of the canals were carried on by Mr. Menocal, who has been the chief engineer of the Nicaragua Canal Construction Company since its organization. His first survey was made in 1872, and the line of the canal as finally located by him runs from Greytown on the Caribbean Sea to Brito on the Pacific coast, by the way of the San Juan River and Lake Nicaragua. Lake Nicaragua is about one hundred miles long, has an average width of about forty-five miles, and is of variable depth, reaching a maximum of 165 feet. The surface of the lake is 110 feet above the sea level. Its western bank approaches within twelve miles of the Pacific, from which it is separated by a divide forty-two feet high.

As concisely described * by Mr. Menocal, "The total distance from ocean to ocean by sailing line through canal and lake is 169.45 miles, of which but 26.78 miles will be wholly in excavation, the other 142.67 miles being through Lake Nicaragua, the San Juan River and artificial basins. Of the latter distance, 102 miles will have a depth of thirty feet or more, requiring neither dredging nor excavation. The lake is the main feeder and the summit level of the canal. It is connected with the Pacific Ocean by 11.40 miles of canal in excavation and 5.27 miles of artificial basin created in the valley of Tola by the construction of a dam across a narrow gorge of the valley, three miles distant from the Pacific coast. From the lake eastward the canal follows the San Juan River for a distance of 64½ miles to Ochoa, where by the construction of a dam across the river the surface of the water is raised

* *Cf.* Senate Report No. 1944, Fifty-first Congress, second session, pp. :70, 171, statement of A. G. Menocal.

fifty-five feet and slack-water navigation secured along that distance, converting that portion of the river into an extension of the lake. Just above the dam the canal leaves the bed of the river and enters into a chain of artificial basins formed by the construction of a series of dams and embankments and short cuts, confining and connecting adjacent valleys (of the San Francisco Creek) for a distance of about twelve miles to the western end of the great divide cut. The heaviest work in the whole line is now encountered in crossing the divide separating the valleys of the San Francisco and Deseado Creeks, where nearly eleven million cubic yards of rock and earth excavation are concentrated in a distance of two and three-fourths miles. However, the rock is hard and homogeneous, there are ample natural facilities for doing the work; the rock is needed for the construction of breakwaters, locks, dams, embankments, etc., and if not found in that favorable centre of distribution it would have to be quarried at other places. Easterly of the divide cut there is another artificial basin about five miles long, formed by the construction of a dam across the valley of the Deseado, and thence twelve miles of canal in excavation extending to the harbor of Greytown, of which nearly ten miles will be at the level of the sea. The summit level of the canal extends from the western end of the basin of Tola to the eastern end of the Deseado basin, a distance of 154 miles. It has been stated that this upper level is 110 feet above the sea level. This elevation is proposed to be overcome by six locks, three on the Atlantic and three on the Pacific slopes—the lifts of these locks varying from a maximum of forty-five feet to a minimum of twenty-five feet, their uniform length being 650 feet and the width eighty feet. The harbors of Greytown and Brito need to be enlarged and improved by the construction of breakwaters and by dredging, but the works required present no serious engineering difficulties. With the exception of the rock cuts in the eastern and western divides, the canal prism will be at all points wide enough for two ships to travel in opposite directions, and its least depth will be thirty feet. In the lake, the river San Juan and the artificial basins vessels can travel in entire freedom."

As estimated by Mr. Menocal the actual cash cost of the canal will be $65,000,000; English engineers, to whom the estimates were submitted for revision, raised the maximum to $87,000,000. It will, of course, take six or seven years to construct the canal, and the interest on the capital will bring the real cost up to $100,000,000; there is little doubt but that the enterprise could be carried through for that money were the credit of the company that constructs the waterway as good as that of the United States. No private company has such good credit, and if the Maritime Canal Company of Nicaragua carries the work through to completion its obligations will represent much more than $100,000,000. They would certainly be twice that, and would probably be more. The capital stock of the Maritime Canal Company is $100,000,000, and it is allowed to issue bonds to the amount of $150,000,000. The Nicaragua Canal Construction Company agreed to construct the canal for the Maritime Company and to accept as a remuneration the $150,000,000 of the Maritime Company's bonds and all its stock. The available residue of the stock is $80,500,000; for of the $100,000,000, $6,000,000 went to Nicaragua and $1,500,000 to Costa Rica, and $12,000,000 to the construction company, to pay for the concessions. The construction company will doubtless raise the funds for the work by selling the bonds more or less below par, throwing in the stock to the purchasers as a bonus.

The work of construction has been in progress since June, 1889. Up to January 1, 1893, there had been $6,885,230.33 expended on the enterprise, of which sum, $2,648,343.81 were paid out between December 15, 1890, and January 1, 1893. The work thus far has been done at and near Greytown, and consists of the construction of a breakwater, the dredging of the harbor, the building of a railroad from Greytown across the marshes and the beginning of the excavation of the channel across this low-lying plain from Greytown to the foot hills.

By chartering the Maritime Canal Company of Nicaragua, in 1889, Congress gave up, for the present, the construction of the canal directly by the United States: but this action failed to satisfy many of those who appreciate the real political and economic significance of the waterway to the United States. By a resolution of the Senate, April 11, 1890, the Committee on Foreign Relations was "directed to inquire into what steps have been taken under the act of Congress entitled 'An Act to Incorporate the Maritime Canal Company of Nicaragua' approved 20th February, 1889, and what are the present conditions and prospects of the enterprise; and to consider and report what, in its opinion, the interests of the United States may require in respect of that interoceanic communication." The committee took testimony from Mr. Miller, Mr. Menocal, Mr. Hotchkiss and Mr. A. T. Mason, Attorney of the Nicaragua Canal Construction Company. This testimony, together with a good deal of other information regarding the canal, accompanied the report made by the committee January 10, 1891.* The bill framed by the committee for the purpose of limiting the obligations of the Maritime Canal Company to the actual cost of the work by granting the company the credit of the United States was not only reported too late for action, but did not satisfy the Senate. A second resolution, dated January 7, 1892, directed the committee to inquire what progress had been made with the work, what stocks had been disposed of, what contracts had been made by the company, and to investigate the interests of the United States in the proposed interoceanic communication.

The testimony† taken pursuant to this second resolution resulted, at the last session of Congress, in the introduction into the Senate of a bill differing from the former one in some details. Its chief provisions were: The United States was to endorse the bonds of the Maritime Company to an amount not to exceed $100,000,000; the bonds were to date from January 1, 1893, to bear interest at three per cent per annum from date of issue, to be redeemable after 1913, and to mature in 1953. The stock of the Maritime Company was to remain at $100,000,000, of which $6,000,000 was reserved to Nicaragua and $1,500,000 to Costa Rica for

---

* Senate Report 1944, Fifty-first Congress, second session.
† Senate Report 1262, Fifty-second Congress, second session, Feb, 4, 1893.

their concessions, and $12,000,000 was to remain in the ownership of those who had purchased the stock from the Maritime Company ;* the remainder of the stock, $80,500,000, was to pass into the absolute ownership of the United States without liability to further payment or assessment. The bill provided for a sinking fund of $1,000,000 per annum, to be invested in the bonds of the Maritime Company, or in good securities at three per cent interest. It was assumed by the committee that the tonnage passing through the canal would average 9,000,000 tons a year during the first twenty years (it would probably be more) ; a toll of a dollar a ton would therefore yield $9,000,000 a year. This would pay the interest on $100,000,000 ($3,000,000), pay the cost of maintenance and operation (about $1,800,000), and leave $4,200,000 for the stockholders. On this basis the revenue of the United States from the canal would pay off the entire cost of the waterway in less than twenty years. The bill provided that the expenditures of the company for works of construction were to be submitted to a board of United States engineers for criticism. The canal, when constructed, was to be under the management of a board of fifteen directors, ten of whom were to be appointed by the President of the United States and confirmed by the Senate. Of the other five, the President, voting the stock of the United States, by his proxy, was to choose two.

The bill did not come to a vote, partly because it was debated so late in the session, February 13 and 14, but also because of the strong feeling that the United States ought to construct the canal herself, the same as is done in the case of other waterways. The action that the government is to take for the promotion of the enterprise is still an unsettled question, to the solution of which the Fifty-third Congress ought to bend its best effort.

Whether the United States assumes direct and entire charge of the construction of the canal, or brings the Maritime

* *Vide Supra* pp. 137-38.

Canal Company completely under control and allows the company to proceed with the work strengthened by the credit of the government, is a question of secondary importance. In one way or the other the United States ought to promote the enterprise. The government can carry through the work far more economically than can any corporation of individuals. The State can construct the canal for $100,000,000; no corporation can do it for less than $200,000,000. The burden of extra cost must, of course, fall chiefly on our trade and industries. Notice what the difference in the fixed charges would be in the two cases: Were the United States to construct the canal, or loan its credit for the purpose, the annual fixed charges would be, interest at three per cent on $100,000,000, $3,000,000; maintenance, repairs and operation probably less than (but we will say) $2,000,000; for a sinking fund which invested at three per cent would amortize the principal in fifty years, $1,000,000, total fixed charges, $6,000,000. Now, compare this with the fixed charges that a corporation would have to bear: Interest at six per cent on $200,000,000, $12,000,000; maintenance, repairs and operation, $2,000,000; total fixed charges, exclusive of amortization of capital, $14,000,000. The fixed charges have to be met by tolls. If there be 9,000,000 tons a year passing the canal, a toll of one dollar a ton would yield $9,000,000. This sum would meet the fixed charges in case the Government constructs the canal or loans its credit for the purpose, and leave $3,000,000 for distribution among shareholders; but a toll of a dollar a ton would come $5,000,000 short of meeting the fixed charges that a corporation would have to bear; while a toll of $2.00 a ton would yield only a two per cent dividend. A toll of $2.50 a ton would yield only four and one-eighth per cent dividend, and a toll as high as that would be an exclusive one for some kinds of bulky freight.

The government could make the toll less than a dollar a ton as the traffic on the waterway increased, indeed could reduce the tolls, after the capital invested had been amortized, so that they would simply cover fixed charges. More than this, the government might adjust the tolls so as to favor our coast-wise trade. We would be obliged to levy the same toll on our ships engaged in the foreign trade as we laid on vessels of other countries; but the coast-wise traffic might be given the free use of the canal.

Furthermore, with the aid of the State, the canal can be constructed, and its benefits realized much sooner. Should the United States be apathetic the project will not fail. "It will be worked out; we cannot help it. This generation of men may hesitate and halt and falter about it, but there will come another along who will take it up and work it out."* American enterprise and genius will, in time, overcome the difficulties and obstacles, though the enterprise be left to individual effort; however, this work of widest national importance ought not to be delayed and made a needlessly heavy burden on commerce, trade and industry, but should receive the prompt and efficient support of the State.

NOTE.

After Chapter XII. had been given final form by the printer, the morning papers of August 31, 1893, gave notice that, on the day previous, the Nicaragua Canal Construction Company had been obliged to go into the hands of a receiver, Mr. Thomas B. Atkins, secretary and treasurer of the Maritime Canal Company. The Construction Company, it appears, has been embarrassed for some time, and not very much work has been done since January 1, 1893. There are several reasons for the financial embarrassment of the company. Of course the chief one is the crisis that has so thoroughly crippled business. As Warner Miller, the president of the Construction Company, says : "During all the present financial difficulties it has been trying to get money to carry the work of construction along. The hard times have rendered

* Speech by Senator Morgan in the Senate, February 13, 1893.

it substantially impossible to get subscriptions to keep things moving." The financial crisis has weakened the Construction Company by the financial losses it has brought upon certain members that were largely interested in the company. Furthermore, the Panama scandal has tended to lessen the confidence of capitalists in the success of the Nicaragua Canal. The recent war in Nicaragua has retarded the work, and has probably made the receivership necessary earlier than it would otherwise have been.

Whether the construction of the canal will be interrupted very long or not is impossible to foretell. Mr. Miller says: "It ought not to. The Maritime Company, to which the concessions were made, will remain intact. It is unimpaired, and ought to be able, after times improve, to revive the enterprise and go ahead with it." It is quite probable that the re-organized Construction Company or some other private association of men will resume the work of construction after a short time ; but, without venturing to prophesy, I feel confident that the ultimate assumption of the enterprise by the United States will come sooner, because of the delays that come to the execution of the work by private corporation. The canal is of too vital importance to be very long delayed.

CHAPTER XIII.
THE ECONOMIC SIGNIFICANCE TO THE UNITED STATES OF THE EXTENSION OF INLAND WATERWAYS.

The improvement and extension of inland waterways alter industrial, commercial and social conditions. The significance of cheap transportation has been but briefly referred to in the previous pages. The closing chapter of a monograph written, as this is, in the hope of showing how waterways conduce to cheapen the cost of carriage and to develop industry, ought, from the nature of the subject treated, to emphasize strongly the economic importance of inland navigation, to direct attention especially to the industrial, commercial and social interests of the United States and to show how they may be modified by the further extension of water routes.

The industry that lies at the basis of all others is agriculture, and its dependence on the conditions of transportation is most vital. Indeed, the farmer is especially at the mercy of those who control the shipment of freight. His produce must, in large part, be moved during a few months of the year, a fact of which the railroads take advantage by raising rates when produce is being moved.

The agricultural development of the States north of the Ohio and east of the Mississippi has been phenomenal. Bordering on an inland waterway of unparalleled value, fourteen hundred miles long and connected with the seaboard by a navigable river and a canal, that have furnished cheap rates for a part of the freight and have regulated all charges by rail, they have marketed their farm produce on the seaboard and across the ocean.* Kansas, Nebraska and the Dakotas, though possessing soil superior to that of the Lake States for the growth of several kinds of grain, are at

---

* Even such a bulky article as hay is shipped to Europe. The farmers of Wisconsin, even, are this year marketing hay in France, shipment being entirely by water. One Fond du Lac hay buyer shipped $65,000 worth in June, 1893.

a great disadvantage as compared with them, because of the high rates of transportation by rail. It is not because the Dakotas are farther from New York and Liverpool than Minnesota, Wisconsin and Illinois are, that the former States are so much at a disadvantage; had they such a waterway as the Great Lakes available for use, their greater distance from the seaboard markets and from the mines and forests that supply them with fuel and lumber would be of small moment. The extension of the commerce of the Great Lakes to St. Paul and Minneapolis and the further improvement of the Missouri and Mississippi Rivers and their better connection with the lakes will give the agriculture of the west Mississippi States a great impetus. If in addition to securing better means of transportation these States can find ample coal beds within their borders, they will rank second to none of the States in their industrial prosperity.

The agricultural interests of the Mississippi Valley will be largely promoted by the Nicaragua Canal. It will continue the water route, beginning with the Missouri, Ohio and the upper Mississippi, to the harbors of San Francisco, Portland, Callao and Valparaiso, where the prairies of the United States will then market their produce. The agricultural interests of the Pacific slope will be greatly forwarded by the Nicaragua Canal. Take the single item of wheat and flour, of which 1,800,000 tons were shipped from the Pacific States to Europe in 1891. The canal would have saved $2.00 a ton, or $3,600,000 in freight charges. Under present conditions for marketing the produce of the Pacific States, the amount grown is far less than it would be with the Nicaragua Canal open for traffic. The wheat crop of Washington last year is estimated at 20,000,000 bushels, but the capacity of the cereal-growing lands of the State is about 200,000,000 bushels (6,000,000 tons).*

The benefits of inland waterways to agriculture manifest themselves in a more local and specific way. There are

* *Cf.* Speech by Senator Squire, *Congressional Record*, February 15, 1893, p. 1676

many articles of comparatively small value for which transportation by rail is possible only to limited quantities and for short distances. Cheap transportation by water increases the marketable quantities of such subsidiary farm products as fertilizers, clay, sand, straw, hay and wood. The byproducts, as is the case with manufacture, are often the real source of the farmer's profit; if they are marketable, much more land becomes possible of cultivation, population increases and the value of land rises.

The water routes of the United States have, to a large degree, made possible the development of our iron industries. Some of the richest iron regions of the United States, those of northern Michigan and Wisconsin, lie nearly a thousand miles from the great coal fields of Pennsylvania, but with a waterway connecting them, on which freight rates are only a little over a mill a ton mile, the two mining regions are brought close together. They are able, because of this fact, to compete with the newly-opened mines of the South that lie next door to the rich coal beds of Alabama.

The distribution and consumption of coal, both for manufacturing and heating purposes, have been made much greater in the United States because of inland transportation; nor have we by any means yet reached the limit of the possibilities of wider distribution or lower prices. The distribution of Pennsylvania coal by means of the Ohio River and the Great Lakes will increase in the future with the improvement and extension of the water routes of the Great Lakes and the Mississippi River system. The improvement of the Missouri, the construction of a river-ship canal between the Mississippi River and Lake Michigan, of lake-ship canals from Pittsburgh to Lake Erie and from Lake Superior to St. Paul and Minneapolis, will cheapen coal throughout the North and West, and greatly widen the present marketable limits.

By the improvements of the Tombigbee and Warrior rivers, now in process of execution, the coal from the rich mines of upper Alabama is going to secure a wide market. Labor is cheap, and the coal can be so easily mined that, when the canalization of the rivers is completed, coal can be delivered on shipboard at Mobile for a dollar and twenty-five cents a ton. From Mobile it can be carried to the ports of the Gulf, up the rivers of the lower Mississippi Valley, and, on the completion of the Nicaragua Canal, to our Pacific States and to the western shores of South America. In the markets of the western slope of South America coal now sells from nine to twelve dollars a ton.*

Inland waterways are likewise of great importance to the producers and consumers of lumber in the United States. Though the timber is widely distributed, there are nevertheless vast regions into which all lumber has to be imported; furthermore, the two greatest lumber districts of the United States, Northern Wisconsin and Michigan, and the States of Washington and Oregon are far distant from the prairies of the Mississippi Valley and the manufacturing cities of the Eastern States. The forests of Wisconsin and Michigan being situated between the headwaters of the Great Lakes and the Mississippi are able to distribute their lumber cheaply by means of these great waterways to widely remote markets. Not so the forests of the Pacific slope, whose markets are at present almost exclusively limited to the region west of the Rockies. That part of Washington alone which lies west of the Cascade Range contains 20,000,000 acres of timber, on which there are 400,000,000,000 feet of salable lumber, but only a few kinds of this lumber can pay the costs of transportation East. Masts and spars are now shipped around the Horn, and of late some Eastern wagon manufacturers have had special grades of lumber brought by the same long route. Thus far the railroads have been able to transport east from Washington only high grade cedar shingles. It is probable that kiln-dried lumber is the only kind that can be shipped from the Pacific States by rail to

* From speech by Senator Frye, in the Senate, February 13, 1893.

the Mississippi Valley.* The Nicaragua Canal will bring this vast wealth of lumber in the Western States 10,000 miles nearer market, greatly increase its sale and add largely to the value of the standing timber.

Inland waterways enable home industries to compete more easily with foreign producers, not only by decreasing the costs of transporting articles destined for exportation, but also by making raw materials cheaper. The ways in which the waterways do and might lower the costs of the products of the farms, mines and forests of the United States have been noted. A country such as the United States, in which a high standard of life among laborers fixes the necessary rate of wages high and in which capital demands a high rate of interest, can compete with a country, where the standard of life and wages are lower, only by virtue of the superior productive power of labor and by having cheaper raw materials. Now, whatever lessens the cost of raw materials allows the price of finished goods to fall by a like amount without trenching on the amount received by wages and interest, wages being here used to include remuneration for intelligence. The development of the inland navigation of the United States will assist us in maintaining the higher standard of life in competition with Europe.

Suppose again, that the waterways lower the cost of raw materials entering into consumption goods produced in industries where competition does not exist or is present in only a slight degree. Competition does not then compel the lowering of price and the lower cost for raw materials leaves a larger portion of the value of the finished products for wages and interest.† The wage-earners have a direct interest

* *Cf.* Speech by Senator Squire in the Senate, February 14, 1893.
† Patten, "The Premises of Political Economy," p. 107: "If five bushels of wheat and ten pounds of cotton are consumed in the production of one hundred yards of cloth, wages and interest will depend on the value of wheat and cotton.' While twenty yards of cloth will exchange for the above amount of wheat and cotton, eighty yards will remain to be distributed as wages and interest, but as the value of wheat and cotton increases so that thirty, then forty or more, of the hundred yards of cloth must be given in exchange for them, the return for labor and capital is reduced by a like amount. It is then the margin between the value of what is consumed in production and what is produced, on which wages and interest depend, and they increase as the margin is enlarged."

in the cheapening of transportation of raw materials by means of inland waterways. The cheapening of raw materials increases the net, or surplus, value of the finished product above the costs of production; to whom this larger surplus value will go—*i. e.*, whether to the wage-earners or the capitalists, and in what proportion—depends on the relative strength of these two agents of production.* If the laborers have a firm standard of life and the desire to raise it, they will secure a large part of the savings due to cheaper raw materials. Inland waterways, by reducing the cost of production, so affect industry as to put laborers under objective economic conditions that make it easier for them to raise their standard of living.

Intimately connected with the influence of inland waterways on industrial development are their effects on domestic and foreign commerce. A large part of this monograph has been devoted to the consideration of the function of inland waterways as promoters of domestic commerce, and little further need be said on that theme. The numerous works for the improvement and extension of inland waterways that have been, or now are, the objects of appropriation, might be considered and note made of the commerce that has been, and is being, developed as the result of the liberality of Congress; but this would needlessly multiply illustrations of the same general character as those have which have already been given.†

Mention has been made of several unfinished works and of others whose execution is proposed, the effect of which must surely be a large increase of our inland navigation. Past improvements of the Mississippi, the Ohio, the Hudson, the Great Lakes and other important waterways have been the sesame of valuable commerce, but what has as yet been revealed is only the forecast of future possibilities.

---

* "The Stability of Prices," by S. N. Patten.

† In the reports of the chief of engineers each object of appropriation is discussed at length. The report of the Senate Committee on Commerce, May 13, 1893, gives this information in briefer form.

EXTENSION OF INLAND WATERWAYS. 153

A great increase in the domestic commerce of the United States awaits the construction of the Nicaragua Canal. Only when the waterway shall have broken through the barrier which the Rocky Mountains oppose to the communication of the Eastern with the Western commonwealths will our country become in a commercial sense the United States.

The Nicaragua Canal will give a powerful impetus to the trade of the United States with foreign countries. The great influence of the Suez Canal on the commerce of the nations of Europe, especially England, is well known. According to the report of the Suez Canal Company, published June 2, 1892, 4207 ships passed the canal the previous year, seventy-six per cent of the vessels sailing under the English flag. Of the total tonnage, 8,698,770 tons, England's share was seventy-eight per cent. England's commerce with the East has risen from $537,000,000 in 1870, at the opening of the canal, to $752,000,000 in 1887, a gain of over forty per cent in seventeen years. The increase of England's total commerce with the world during this time was only seventeen per cent.†

The United States will receive greater benefit from the Nicaragua Canal than England has gained from the waterway across the isthmus of Suez. The water route through Nicaragua will give the Pacific States European markets and the Eastern cities of the United States trade with nations bordering on the Pacific, while the Gulf States will derive especial benefit. As the Atlantic States face the east and look across the ocean to Europe, so the Gulf States face the south and look with longing eyes across the isthmus to the markets of the Western States, of South America and of Japan.

The Suez Canal has been a positive detriment to our foreign commerce, in that it has given England the incontestable supremacy in the trade with China, Japan and Australia. Before the construction of the canal we were as

† See Warner Miller, *Engineering Magazine*, March, 1893.

near these ports as England; now we are 2700 miles farther distant. Let the Nicaragua Canal be opened and this will be reversed. The United States will then be as near Hong Kong as Liverpool, while we shall be 1200 miles nearer than Liverpool to the northern ports of China. We shall be 2700 miles nearer the western ports of South America, 1900 miles nearer to Japan and 1000 miles nearer Australia.*

The commerce with the countries of the Pacific is well worth our effort to obtain. These countries—China, Japan, Australia, Tasmania, New Zealand, Hawaii, Ecuador, Bolivia, Peru, Chile, etc.—have a total commerce equal to $1,215,004,956, of which the imports are valued at $642,361,745 and the exports at $572,543,211. In the distribution of this trade, England and the United States share as follows: Great Britain sells goods to the value of $467,016,507 and buys to the amount of $346,550,882. Thus the balance in England's favor is $120,465,625. The value of the goods sold by the United States is $41,511,362, of those bought, $64,003,920, leaving a balance against us of $22,492,558.† We can get most of this trade when the Nicaragua Canal is put through. Last year China imported cotton and cotton goods to the value of $61,504,348, and the United States furnished only $5,360,508 of this; England supplied most of the rest by means of cotton purchased from us. The first shipment of cotton from the United States to

---

* The following table shows the number of miles that the Nicaragua Canal will shorten the distances between several important ports:

New York to—	Miles.	New Orleans to—	Miles	Liverpool to—	Miles.
San Francisco	9,894	San Francisco	11,005	New Zealand	1,051
Hong Kong	4,163	Guayaquil	9,343	Hong Kong	1,265
Yokohama	6,827	Callao	7,913	Yokohama	3,929
Melbourne	3,290	Valparaiso	5,975	Guayaquil	5,431
New Zealand	3,870	Liverpool to—		Callao	4,090
Sandwich Islands,	7 842	San Francisco	6,996	Valparaiso	2,114
Callao	6,985	Melbourne	391	Sandwich Islands,	4,944
Valparaiso	5,062				

Taken from the Senate Report, 1142, Fifty-second Congress, second session. It will be noted that the saving in distance is without exception in favor of the United States.

† See *Congressional Record*, February 14, 1893. Speech by Senator Frye.

Japan was in 1888, when 85,000 pounds were sent. In 1891 7,000,000 pounds were sent to supply 380,000 spindles. The industrial development of the Orient must surely follow the introduction of better means of inland communication. This industrial revolution has as yet but begun. If we are in possession of a water route across Nicaragua we shall greatly benefit by the growth that the foreign trade of the Pacific States is to experience in the future. The Orient and the Occident are now separated from each other by the mountain wall that skirts the coast of America from Alaska to the Strait of Magellan. At Nicaragua this wall is only a few feet high. Twenty-six miles of excavation at this point will make a waterway from ocean to ocean. When once this way is constructed the East and the West will be united by the close bonds of commercial amity, we shall send iron and steel to the nations beyond the Pacific, we shall sell them locomotives, engines and other machinery with which to build their railroads and telegraphs and to establish and develop their manufacturing industries. The Nicaragua Canal will be the highway through which the civilization of America will pass to the peaceful conquest of the East.

Reference has been made in the introductory chapter and in this to the fact that the extension of inland waterways is of social, as well as industrial, significance. Economic forces combine with moral ones in social reform. Rapid transportation and cheap freight rates condition to a large degree all industrial activity. It is with cheap transportation only that this monograph has concerned itself; but to the extent that waterways have been shown to cheapen rates to that extent have they been shown to be an economic force that makes for social reform.

Inland waterways operate indirectly to promote social reform. The regeneration of the dependent classes will be brought about directly by the influences that work to change the subjective nature of the men in the lower strata of society.

Of course, the fundamental forces by which this can be accomplished must be subjective and psychic, but these can be efficient in a large degree only when the objective conditions are made as favorable as possible. Society, the State and capital in its organized forms have an important duty to perform in setting in order the theatre in which the moral, the psychic forces must act.

If the thesis of this monograph has been established, the extension of inland waterways has an important bearing on the social as well as the industrial problems of the day, and it is an incomplete view of the present functions of inland navigation that reveals only their commercial and industrial aspects. To the extent that the power of cheap transportation to promote social reform is realized will the striking words of the Cullom Committee acquire significance: "The manifest destiny of our country points unerringly to this *emancipation of the waters* as its next great work, a fitting sequel to the emancipation of the slave, a destiny not of war, but of beneficence and peace, to which the heart of the nation turns as spontaneously and resistlessly as the waters of its great river flow to the Gulf." The figure of speech is a strong one, it is true, but it serves well to emphasize an important truth by expressing the hope of the present in a prophecy for the future.

BIBLIOGRAPHY OF WORKS CONSULTED.

ACWORTH, W. M.—Article in *Contemporary Review*, Sept., 1891.
English and American Railways. *Engineering Magazine*, May, 1893.
The Railways and the Traders, a Sketch of the Railway Rates Question. London, 1891.
ADAMS, C. F.—Railroads, Their Origins and Problems. New York, 1878.
ADAMS, H. B.—The Potomac Company, The Johns Hopkins University Studies.
ADAMS, H. M.—Outline Map of the United States, Showing the Tonnage of the Rivers and Harbors. Washington, 1890.
ADAMS, JOHN QUINCY—Second Message to Congress.
Almanach de Gotha. Paris.
Annales des Ponts et Chaussées. Paris.
Annuaire Statisque de la France. Paris.
ARTHUR, CHESTER A.—Veto Message on the River and Harbor Bill of 1882. American Cyclopædia Annual. 1882. p. 148.
BELLINGRATH, EWALD—Studien über Bau und Betrieb eines deutschen Kanalnetzes. Berlin, 1879.
BENTON, THOMAS H.—Abridgement of Debates of Congress.
Thirty Years' View; or, a History of the Working of the American Government for Thirty Years, from 1820-1850. 2 vols. New York, 1861, 1862.
BIDDLE, T. G.—The Future World's Highway, The East and West Waterway. *Engineering Magazine*, June, 1892.
BLANCHE and YMBERT—Dictionnaire de l'Administration Française; the article on Travaux Publics.
BLOCK, MAURICE—Annuaire de l'Économie politique et de la Statistique. Paris, 1892.
Dictionnaire de l'Aministration Française; article on Travaux Publics
BOLLES, A. S.—Financial History of the United States. 3 vols. New York.
BOURNE, E. G.—A History of the Surplus of 1837. Questions of the Day No. 24. New York. 1885.
CARNEGIE, ANDREW—Triumphant Democracy, Chapter XIII on Railways and Waterways. 1888.
CLARK, F. C.—State Railroad Commissions, and How they May be Made Effective. Publications of American Economic Association. Vol. VI, No. 6.
COHN, GUSTAV—Untersuchungen über die Englische Eisenbahnpolitik. Vol. I, 1874; vol. II, 1875.
Die Englische Eisenbahnpolitik der letzten Zehn Jahre (1873-1883).
CULLOM, S. M.—Report of the Senate (Cullom) Committee of Investigation, 1885-86. Senate Reports, 1st Sess., 49th Cong. Vol. II.

(157)

CUTTS—Treatise on Party Questions.
DABNEY, W. D.—The Public Regulation of Railways. New York, 1889.
DAVIS, CUSHMAN K.—Our Lake Commerce and Ways to the Sea. *Forum*, February, 1892.
ELLIOT, JONATHAN—Debates in Constitutional Convention. 5 vols. 1891.
ELY, R. T.—Article on Canals in The National Revenues, edited by Albert Shaw. Chicago, 1888.
Eleventh Census of U. S. Statistics of Transportation.
Engineering and Building Record. Vols. XXV, XXVI.
FRYE—Speech in the Senate on the Nicaragua Canal Bill. *Congressional Record*, February 14, 1893.
GALLATIN, ALBERT—Report to Congress, with a paper by Robert Fulton. Senate State Papers, 1st Sess., 14th Cong. Vol. III, No. 19, p. 4. 1815-16.
Scheme of Internal Improvements. *Congressional Record*, April 12, 1808.
HADLEY, A. T.—Railroad Transportation. New York, 1885.
HAMILTON, ALEXANDER—Works of. Vol. I. Report on Manufactures. Philadelphia, 1824.
HANNAN, EDWARD—Annual Reports of the Superintendent of Public Works of the State of New York. 1890, 1891, 1892.
HANSARD—Parliamentary Debates. Speech by Gladstone on Government Control of Railroads. Vol. 76, pp. 480-509 (1844). Speech by Morrison on Governmental Control of Railroads. Vol. 33, pp. 977-88 (1836).
HART, A. B.—The Biography of a River and Harbor Bill. Papers of American Historical Association. Vol. III.
HAUPT, LEWIS M.—Canals and Their Economic Relation to Transportation. Publications American Economic Association. Vol. V, No. 3.
The Commercial Paradox, a paper discussing certain important problems in transportation. Philadelphia, 1888.
v. HOLST, HERMANN—The Constitutional and Political History of the United States (1750-1861). 7 vols. Chicago, 1877-1892.
Interstate Commerce Commission, Second Annual Report of. Washington, 1888.
JACKSON, ANDREW—Messages to Congress. Inaugural Address.
JAMES, E. J.—The Agitation for Federal Regulation of Railways. Publications of the American Economic Association, Vol. II, No. 3.
The Canal and the Railway; Publications of the American Economic Association, Vol. V, No. 3.
JEANS, J. S.—Waterways and Water Transportation in Different Countries. London, 1890.
JEFFERSON, THOMAS—Message to Congress. 1806.
JOHNSON, EMORY R.—River and Harbor Bills. ANNALS OF THE AMERICAN ACADEMY. May, 1892, Vol. II, p. 782. Also Publications of the Academy, No. 58.
JOHNSTON, A.—History of American Politics. New York, 1888.
Internal Improvements. Lalor's Cyclopædia of Political Science, Political Economy and of the Political History of the United States. 3 vols. Chicago, 1883, 1884.

BIBLIOGRAPHY OF WORKS CONSULTED. 159

KUPKA, P. F.—Die Verkehrsmittel in den Vereinigten Staaten. Leipsig, 1883.
Laws of United States Relating to the Improvement of Rivers and Harbors, from August 11, 1790, to March 3, 1887. Sen. Mis. 91, 1887.
MCLEAN, W. T.—Fifty-third Annual Report of the Board of Public Works to the Governor of the State of Ohio for the Year ending November 15, 1891.
MARSHALL, JOHN—Life of Washington. 5 vols. London, 1804.
MEITZEN, AUGUST—Die Kanalfrage in Preussen. *Schmoller's Jahrbuch für Gesetzgebung.* 8 b. 1884.
MERRY, W. L.—The Nicaragua Canal : Its Political Aspects. *Forum*, February, 1892.
MILLER, WARNER—America's Need of the Nicaragua Canal. *Engineering Magazine.* March, 1893.
The Nicaragua Canal and Commerce. *The Forum*, February, 1892.
MORGAN, J. T.—Speech in the Senate on the Nicaragua Canal Bill. *Congressional Record*, February 15, 1893.
MORSE, JOHN T. JR.—John Quincy Adams. American Statesmen Series. Boston, 1882.
NÖRDLING—Selbstkosten der Eisenbahnen und Kanäle. Vienna, 1886.
PATTEN, S. N.—The Premises of Political Economy. Philadelphia, 1885.
The Stability of Prices. Publications of American Economic Association. Vol. III, No. 6.
PEABODY, JAMES—The Necessity for Railway Compacts Under Governmental Regulation. *The Independent*, June 1, 1893.
POOR, H. V.—Manual of the Railroads of the United States. The Volume for the year 1881 contains a sketch of the Rise and Progress of Internal Improvements.
POUTZEN ET J. FLEURY—Voies Navigables et Chemin de Fer. Paris, 1887.
Proceedings of the Deep Waterways Convention, held at Detroit, Mich., December 17 and 18, 1891.
The Public Domain ; Its History, with Statistics. Ex. Doc's. No. 47, 3d Sess., 46th Cong.
Report and Papers of the Fourth and Fifth International Congresses on Inland Navigation. Paris, 1890 and 1892.
Report of the Senate Committee on Commerce. No. 666, 52d Cong., 1st Sess.
Report of the Canadian Department of Railways and Canals for the fiscal year July 1, 1891, to June 30, 1892. Quebec.
Reports of the Chief of Engineers United States Army, 1890, 1891, 1892.
Reports of the Senate Committee on Foreign Relations, No. 1944, 51st Cong., 2d Sess.; No. 1142, 52d Cong. 2d Sess.; No. 1262, 52d Cong. 2d Sess.
Returns made to the Board of Trade in Respect of the Canals and Navigations in the United Kingdom. London, 1888.
RHODES, JAMES F.—History of the United States from the Compromise of 1850. New York, 1893.
River and Harbor Bills. Text of the Bill of September, 1890, and of the Bill approved July 13, 1892.

ROGERS—The Water Route from Chicago to the Ocean. *Scribner's Magazine*, March, 1892.
SAX, EMIL v.—Transport-und Kommunikationswesen. Schönberg's Handbuch der Politischen Oekonomie. Jena, 1890
Die Verkehrsmittel in Volks-und Staatswirtschaft. 2 vols., 1878-1879.
SCHLICHTING, J.—Binnenschiffahrt. *Handwörterbuch der Staatswissenschaften.* Vol. II, p. 628. Jena, 1892.
SCHOULER, JAMES—History of the United States. New York, 1889-91.
SCHURZ, CARL—Life of Henry Clay. American Statesmen Series. Boston, 1887.
SERING—Die landwirtschaftliche Konkurrenz Nord-Amerikas in Gegenwart und Zukunft.
SHERMAN, JOHN—Speech in the Senate on the Nicaragua Canal Bill, *Congressional Record*, February 15, 1893.
SHORT, J. T.—Historical Reference Lists. Columbus, 1882.
MAYO-SMITH and SELIGMAN—Commercial Policy of the United States of America, 1860-1890, in *Schriften des Vereins für Socialpolitik*, XLIX. Leipzig.
SQUIRE, W. C.—Speech in the Senate on the Nicaragua Canal Bill. *Congressional Record.* February 15, 1893.
STAHL—Brennende Fragen zum Bau und Betrieb der Wasserstrassen.
Statesman's Manual, Vols. I, II, III. London.
Statistics of the Railways of the United States. 1890-1891. Washington.
Statistique de la Navigation Interieure de la France. Documents Historiques at Statistiques. Paris.
STEVENS, JOHN A.—Albert Gallatin. American Statesmen Series. Boston, 1884.
STEWART—Report to United States House of Representatives. 19th Cong., 1st Sess., No. 228.
SUMNER, W. G.—Andrew Jackson. American Statesmen Series. Boston, 1882.
SYMPHNER—Transportkosten auf Eisenbahnen und Kanälen. Berlin, 1885.
TANNER, H. S.—Canals and Railroads of the United States. New York, 1840.
Tenth Census of the United States. Vol. IV gives a history of the canals of the United States.
TRAILL, H. D.—Central Government, the Chapter on Board of Trade. London, 1883.
WEBER—Die Wasserstrassen Nord-Europas, England und Schweden.
WEBSTER, SIDNEY—The Diplomacy and Law of the Isthmian Canals. *Harper's Magazine*, Sept., 1893.

INDEX.

Acworth, W. M., crowded condition of passenger traffic in London, 67
Adams, H. M., 16
Annals of the American Academy, 10, 67, 112
Arthur, Chester A., Veto of river and harbor bill of 1882, 118
Atkins, Thomas B., 146

Balize, English settlement at, 135-136; England's treaty with Guatemala in 1859, 136
Bellingrath, Ewald, cost of moving freight by canal, 79; quoted concerning use of hydraulic lifts in Germany, 86; on power of canals to compete with railroads, 88-89
Bibliography of works consulted, 157-160
Bompiani, 104
Brentano, Lujo, on construction of waterways by the State and by corporations, 96-97

Canals, maritime and lake ship-canals characterized, 14-15; should be studied independently of river improvements, 16; length of canals of United States, 32; causes of the abandonment of many canals of New England, Pennsylvania, New York and Ohio, 33-36; traffic on canals: in New England, 31, in France, 42, in Germany, 44; conditions under which canals can compete with railroads, 73-89; classification of, 73; considerations regarding the costs of construction, 74-76; the cost of maintenance, 76-78; of moving freight on, 74-76; use of steam on, 80-81, protection of banks, 81; traction of canal boats, 81-83; large canals more economical, 83-84; Haupt's law, 84; locks on, 84-87; hydraulic lifts and inclined planes, 85-87; Bellingrath on power of canals to compete with railroads, 88-89; use of for draining and irrigating, 88; requisite dimensions, 89; tolls on European waterways, 90; cost of transportation on English waterways, 94; Illinois and Michigan Canal, 124-125; Hennepin Canal, 124; Chicago Drainage Canal, 125; proposed canal from Pittsburg to Lake Erie, 130, from St. Paul to Lake Superior, 130; canal from Great Lakes to the ocean, 131; should be within the United States, 131, 132; proposed canals between Cincinnati and Lake Erie, and between Philadelphia and New York, 132; Nicaragua Canal, 133-146
Chesapeake and Delaware Canal, 129
Chicago Drainage Canal, 125

Chipman, J. L., suggested Detroit waterways convention, 100
Citizens' Municipal Association of Philadelphia, report of 1893, quotation concerning the electric light monopoly of Philadelphia, 50
Clayton-Bulwer Treaty, 135-137
Clements, Edwin, 26-30
Cohn, Gustav, 22
Columbia River, size and resources of region drained, 128; obstructions to navigation, improvements, 128, 129
Combination and consolidation of railroads,—See "Railroads."
Commerce, coastwise and inland of United States, 38; on French waterways, 42, 43; on German waterways, 44, 45; relation between traffic by rail and by water, France, 42, 43, Germany, 45, 46, the United States, 46, 47
Commissions, State railway, 48
Cullom, Shelby M., opposed to pooling contracts, 54; Cullom committee of 1885, 57, 58, 156
Cumberland River, improvements on, 126

Delaunay-Belleville, 70
Detroit, Waterways Convention at, 100
Dufourny, 55, 103

Economic significance of the extension of waterways of the United States, 147-156: I. As regards agriculture, 147-149; II. Iron industries, 149-150; III. Lumber business, 150, 151; IV. Foreign competition, 151, 152; V. Domestic and foreign commerce, 152-155; VI. The promotion of social reform, 6, 151-152, 155-156.
Edmunds, George F., 135
Ely, George H., on a canal from Great Lakes to the sea, 101
England, Waterways of, reasons why they were crippled by the railroads, 23, 24; legislation of Parliament concerning, 24-32; methods employed in improving, 115
Erie Canal, completion of, 32; improvements needed, 35, 36; character of freight on, 40; tonnage on, 46; grain rates on, 55-57; rate per ton mile, 78; boats used on, 78; steam traction on, 81; electric traction on, 83; locks on, 85
Evansville, Waterways convention at, 101
Evarts, William M., 135
Finet, Theophile, quoted concerning rail and water traffic, 39
Fink, Albert, on waterways as regulators of tariffs, 59-60

(161)

Fleury, 43
France, Waterways of, length 41-42; law of 1879, 41; classification and tonnage of freight on, 42; compared with railroads, 42-43; subventions by the departments, 107-108; "navigation chambers, 108; methods by which improvements are made, 115-116
Frye, William P., on opposition to Congressional aid to inland navigation, 10-11; speech in Senate on Nicaragua Canal, 134

Germany, Waterways of, traffic on rivers, 44; on canals, 44-45; statistics of tonnage on, 45; relation to railroads, 45-46; tolls on, 90; State improvement an accepted fact, 96; the way improvements are made, 115-116
Gladstone, William E., quoted concerning power of railroads in Parliament, 25; quotation from speech of 1844 on inefficiency of railway competition, 50
Granger legislation, 48

Hadley, Arthur T., 22
Hannan, Edward, quoted on New York canals, 36; rates on canals and railroads of New York, 56-57; economy of steam traction on Erie Canal, 81
Haupt, Lewis M., relative cost of large and small canals, 75; this stated as a law, 84
Hepburn committee, quoted concerning relation of the canal to the railroad, 59
Hennepin Canal, 124
Hoerschelman, 81
Hotchkiss, Hiram, 138, 142
Hudson River, traffic on, 8; its improvement the charge of the United States, 111; conditions of navigation, improvements, 127
Hydraulic lifts, described, 85; Anderton lift, 86; at Fontinètte and Louvière, 86; suggested for use in Germany and at the Dalles of the Columbia River, Oregon, 86, 129

Illinois and Michigan Canal, 124
Improvement of waterways, arguments for private enterprise, 91-93; for State construction, 93-98; Brentano on, 96-97; chief works should be by the State, 98; facts concerning the United States and the States, 110-111
Inclined planes, described, 85; use on Shropshire Canal, 86; use in Germany and on Morris and Essex Canal, 86; their superiority over locks and lifts, 86-87
Inland navigation, opposition to congressional aid, 9, 11; reasons for present promotion by the State, 11-12; renaissance of, 12-13; international congresses on, 38, 72, 99-100
Internal improvements in the United States, 110, 121; causes of the abandonment of them by Congress from 1830-1870, 112; the River and Harbor Bill, 110-121

International congresses on inland navigation, committee on statistics, appointed by Third Congress, 38; resolution of the Fourth Congress concerning relation of waterways and railroads, 72; the proceedings of the Fourth and Fifth, 99-100
Interstate Commerce, assumption of its control by Congress, 11; the National Commission; its report referred to, 22; the establishment of the commission, 48; it favored pooling, 53; investigation in 1885 of Senate Committee on Interstate Commerce, 57-61; the Commission's freight classification, 59, 60

Jeans, J. Stephen quoted on the use of canals, 36; on locks designed for Nicaragua Canal, 87; on condition of English canals, 93, 94

Kentucky River, length, traffic, improvement of navigation, 125, 126

Lakes, The Great, vessels and traffic on, 8; the commerce compared with the foreign commerce of the United States, 9; tonnage on, 38,47; freight rates compared with charges by rail, 56; the growth of lake commerce has aided the railroads, 68; average freight rate on, 77; costs of transportation on, 77; their improvement not a work adapted to private enterprise, 94, 95; work of Detroit convention to secure twenty-foot channels, 100, 101; convention to discuss a ship-canal to the ocean, 101; no tolls on the Lakes, 106; the twenty-foot channels in, 123; a ship-canal to the ocean, 131; influence of the Great Lakes on the agricultural development of neighboring States, 147, 148
Locks, invention of, 84; impediment to navigation, 85; attempts to substitute lifts and planes, 86, 87; locks on Erie Canal, 85; on Nicaragua Canal, 87, 140; on the Hennepin Canal, 124
Load, relation of net to dead on boats and cars, 77; of an average train, 78, of a boat, 78

Manchester Canal, cost underestimated, 15; cost per mile, 75; its service to commerce, 75
Maritime Canal Company of Nicaragua, 135, 138, 139, 141
Mason, A. T., 142
Mayo-Smith, R., 56
Meitzen, August, 79; quoted on taxing the increment in property resulting from the construction of a waterway, 107
Menocal, A. G., description of Nicaragua Canal, 139, 140; testifies before Senate Committee, 142
Merchants' Exchange of Buffalo, petition to keep the Erie Canal open, 57
Michaelis, estimate of costs of constructing canals in Prussia, 75
Miller, Warner, 137, 138, 142; quoted 145, 146, 153

INDEX. 163

Mississippi River, boats and traffic on, 8; tonnage on, 47; its influence on charges by rail, 57; its improvement should have more reference to control of floods, 94; its improvement is rightly a State enterprise, 94, 95; it is properly a free way, 106; the Mississippi River Commission, 122; the present work of improvement, 122, 123
Minnesota Canal Company, 13, 130
Missouri River, the Missouri River Commission, 123; improvements, 123
Morgan, John T., 134, 146
Morrison, quotation from speech in Parliament, May 17, 1836, 22; resolution introduced in Parliament, 1836, 25; quoted on railway consolidation, 50

Navigation Chambers, proposal to establish them in France, 108
New York Central and Hudson River Railroad, tonnage on, 8; earnings per ton mile, 56; twenty-hour trains from New York to Chicago, 67, 68; expense of moving freight on, 78
Nicaragua Canal, interest in it awakened by the trouble between the United States and Chile, 11; conventions in the interest of, 102; general discussion of, 133-146; three-fold functions of, 133; it should be controlled by the United States, 133, 134, 137, 139, 141, 143, 145; Pres. Hayes quoted on this point, 134; the Clayton-Bulwer Treaty, 135-137; treaty of 1867, 136; proposed treaty of 1884, 136; the Nicaragua Canal Association organized, 137; organization of the Nicaragua Canal Construction Company, 137; concessions of Nicaragua and Costa Rica, 138; the formation of the Maritime Canal Company, 138; beginning of work on Canal, 139; route of canal described by Menocal, 139-140; estimated cost, 140, 141; work done up to January, 1893, 141; Senate investigation in 1890, and bill of 1891, 141, 142; investigation of 1892, 142; bill of 1893, 142, 143; economy of government support of the enterprise, 144, 145; the influence of the canal on the agricultural interests of the Mississippi Valley and Pacific slope, 148; the impetus its construction will give trade and commerce of the United States, 153-155
Nicaragua Canal Association, 137, 138
Nicaragua Canal Construction Company, 137, 138, 139, 141; passes into receiver's hands, 145, 146; probable effect of this, 146
Nord-Ost-See Canal, in process of construction by Prussia and the German Empire, 45; military purpose of, 11

Ohio River, tonnage, 46, 47; the improvement of navigation on, 125; the coal trade on, 149

Panama Canal, cause of failure, 15
Parliament, The English, legislation to maintain waterways independent of railroads, 24-32; futility of such legislation, 24; report of select committee of 1839, 25; power of railway companies over, 25; resolution by Morrison in 1836, 25; bill of 1844, 25; canal owners allowed to become shippers, 26; railway commission from 1847 to 1851, 26; select committee of 1852, 26; bill of 1854, 26, 27; investigation of 1872, 27, 28; bill of 1873, 28; the Railway and Canal Traffic Act of 1888, 29-31; revision of schedule of rates on railways and waterways, 31; operation of law of 1888, 31, 32
Patten, S. N., quoted, 151, 152
Peabody, James, favors pooling, 53
Pennsylvania, Constitution of, Art. XVII, regarding combination of waterways with railroads: quoted, 51; article not enforced, 52
Pennsylvania Railroad, tonnage, 8; earnings per ton mile, expense of conducting transportation, 77, 78
Peslin, 81
Poe, O. M., on deepening channels of the Great Lakes, 123
Pooling contracts, favored by Interstate Commerce Commission, 53; James Peabody on, 53; opposed by Senate Committee, Fifty-second Congress, 54; Senate Committee of Fifty-third Congress to investigate, 54

Railroads, their freight compared with that of waterways, 37-47; influence of waterways on tariffs of, 48-62; differ in character from waterway, 49; combination the natural law of their management, 49-54; Mr. Morrison and Mr. Gladstone on competition among, 49, 50; purpose of English legislation concerning, 51; operation of competition among, 52, 53; pooling discussed, 53, 54; waterways the best regulator of their tariffs, 54; average freight earnings on railroads of United States, 56, compared with rates by water on Great Lakes and Erie Canal, 56, 57; operating expenses in United States, 66, in Germany, 66; cost of conducting transportation on railroads of United States, 78
Railroads and waterways, complementary character of, 64, 69, 70; resolution of the Fourth International Congress on Inland Navigation, 72
Railway Commission of England, from 1847 to 1851, 26; commission re-established in 1878, 28
Reading Railroad, tonnage, 8; expense of moving freight on, 78
Regulation of railroad rates, independent waterway best regulator, 54; Cullom committee on waterways as regulators, 57, 58; volume of freight by water may be less than by rail, 58; wide extent of the influence of the waterway, 59, 60; this extent will increase with growth in unity of charges by rail, 59, 60; small canals have little influence, 60; Van Ornum on waterways as tariff regulators, 58; waterways must be independent of railroads, 61

Revenues of railways, influence of waterways on, 63-72; competition of waterways helpful, 61-66; this shown by statistics of Main from Frankfort to Mayence, 64-66, and by tonnage of railroads near the Great Lakes, 68

River and Harbor Bill, 110-121; first appropriation for harbors, 111; present form of bill, 112; the framing of the bill and its contents, 113-115; section 7 of bill of 1892 quoted, 113; method of executing works, 115; our methods compared with those of England France and Germany, 115, 116; our methods criticised, 116-121; lack of unity of effort and plans, 116; number of works too large, 117; log-rolling, 117-119; its cure, 118; driblet appropriations, 119; these partially abandoned in bills of 1890 and 1892, 119-121; the bill has been too harshly criticised, 121

Rhodes, James F., 135
Roberts, Thomas P., 7, 66, 80, 130.

Sax, Emil v., 109
St. Paul, proposed canal from Great Lakes to, 95, 149
Schlichting, Julius 45, 81
Seligman, E. R. A., 56
Sering, M., 57, 66
Sherman, John, 135
Squire, Watson C., 148, 151
State railroads, the relation of waterways to, 70-72; this relation in Prussia, 97; surplus earnings ought not to go into the State's general budget, 105; division of costs of construction in Prussia between central and local governments, 109
Stahl, 39
Supervision of waterways by the State, the necessary extent of, 98
Symphner, cost of freight by canal, 79; quoted, 88
Ships, their cost relatively to cars, 78
Standard of life, influence of cheap and rapid transit on, 6, 7, 151, 152, 155, 156
Steamboats, kinds used on rivers, 82; use of chain and screw steamers on waterways, 82

Tennessee River, conditions of navigation, improvements, 126, 127
Tolls, on waterways of France, Italy, Belgium, Holland, England, the United States, New York, Illinois and Ohio, 103; their abolition has aided navigation, 104; the four principles according to which tolls may be assessed, 104, 105; an undesirable form of taxation, 105; the law according to which tolls should be levied, 105; the application of the law, 106-109; taxing the increment, 107, 108; abolition of tolls on all waterways not necessary, 109

Traction of boats, difficulties in the way of steam traction on canals, 80-82; electric traction, 83; by locomotives, 83

Trade, dependence on transportation, 7; foreign trade of the United States compared with inland navigation, 9

Transportation, importance of the study of, 5, 6; social and industrial effects of cheap rates, 6-9, 151, 152, 155, 156; economic effects of cheap transportation, 147-155

Union for the improvement of the canals of the State of New York, centennial convention of 1892, 101
United States, waterways of, See "Waterways;" waterways being constructed, 122-129; proposed waterways, 129-132

Van der Borght, 46; quoted, 69
Van der Sleyden, 81
Van Ornum, John L., quoted on waterways as tariff regulators, 58

Washington, Convention at, to consider project of a larger canal from Great Lakes to the ocean, 101
Waterways, tonnage on Great Lakes, 8; Mississippi River, 8, Hudson River, 8; few improvements during several decades, 9; military significance of, 11, 12; classification of, 14, 15; the way they should be studied, 16-19; present condition of English and American, 20-36; this accounted for, 20, 21; struggle of English railways with, 22-32, length and ownership of English, 29; traffic on English, 31; condition of waterways of the United States, 32-36; manner of collecting statistics of traffic on, 37, 38; statistics of traffic classified, United States, 38, France, 42; kinds of freight adapted to carriage on, 38-40; nature of freight on waterways, 40, 41, of France, 41-43, of Germany, 44-46; effect of dissimilarity of dimensions in traffic on, 41-43; they are public highways, 49; regulators of railroad tariffs, 54-62; costs of moving freight on, 77-79; interruptions to navigation on, 87, 88; improvement of by the State and by corporations, 90-102; arguments for private enterprise, 91-93; for State construction, 93-99; present study of the functions of, 99-102; tolls on, 103-109; methods employed by the United States to improve them, 110-121; leading waterways of United States, 122-129; proposed works, 129-132; economic significance to the United States of the extension of, 147-156.

www.ingramcontent.com/pod-product-compliance
Lightning Source LLC
Chambersburg PA
CBHW030253170426
43202CB00009B/728